Ethiopian Airlines
The African Aviation Powerhouse

JOZEF MOLS

AIRLINES SERIES, VOLUME 2

Contents page image: Ethiopian Airlines Boeing 720B. (Thys Postma collection)

Published by Key Books
An imprint of Key Publishing Ltd
PO Box 100
Stamford
Lincs PE19 1XQ

www.keypublishing.com

The right of Jozef Mols to be identified as the author of this book has been asserted in accordance with the Copyright, Designs and Patents Act 1988 Sections 77 and 78.

Copyright © Jozef Mols, 2021

ISBN 978 1 80282 002 7

All rights reserved. Reproduction in whole or in part in any form whatsoever or by any means is strictly prohibited without the prior permission of the Publisher.

Typeset by SJmagic DESIGN SERVICES, India.

Contents

Introduction and Acknowledgements 4
Chapter 1   Early Days of Aviation 7
Chapter 2   Start Up with American Help 12
Chapter 3   The Jet Age 20
Chapter 4   Profits and Taxes in a Marxist Country 28
Chapter 5   Aggressive Expansion 36
Chapter 6   'Vision 2025' 44
Chapter 7   Pan-African Vision Pays Off 54
Chapter 8   Zambian Adventure 59
Chapter 9   Expanding the African Footprint 65
Chapter 10 'Pitch Up, Pitch Up' 71
Chapter 11 The COVID-19 Pandemic 77
Appendix 1 Incidents and Accidents 85
Appendix 2 Ethiopian Airlines Fleet Details 91
Appendix 3 Notes and References 93

Introduction and Acknowledgements

When I was a schoolboy, my mother used to stimulate my school results by giving me books each time I came home with good marks. And, as I was a good student, my library started growing and growing. My preference was for books regarding foreign countries and nature, a passion I still have today. One particular book – with many photos – gave me a first impression of Ethiopia and its enormous cultural heritage. Unfortunately, other photos later appeared in the press, showing children and adults dying of hunger during the long periods of famine and civil war that would ravage the country.

A few years ago, I had the pleasure of organising and guiding a safari for my photography club in South Africa. We decided to fly with Ethiopian Airlines from Brussels via Addis Ababa to Johannesburg. When boarding the plane, I thought back to my very first impressions of Ethiopia, the book my mother gave me and the subsequent photos I saw in the media. I wanted to understand how it was possible for Ethiopian Airlines, an airline born in 1946 in a poor country ravaged by recent history, to become the leading airline in Africa and one of the most successful airlines in the world. That is how I started my investigations, which ultimately would result in this book.

Ethiopia – officially the Federal Democratic Republic of Ethiopia – is a fascinating landlocked country in the Horn of Africa. It shares borders with Eritrea to the north, Djibouti and Somalia to the northeast, Sudan to the northwest and Kenya to the south. With a population of over 110 million inhabitants, it is one of the most populous countries in the world. The oldest hominid discovered in Ethiopia to date is the 4.2-million-year-old *Ardipithecus ramidus*, found in 1994. Ethiopia has often been considered as one of the earliest sites of the emergence of modern humans. Archaeological evidence indicates that Ethiopia was once the region from which modern humans set out for the Middle East and places beyond, although other scholars suggest – based on linguistic studies – that the Afroasiatic-speaking populations arrived in Ethiopia from the Nile Valley. Around the 8th century BCE, a kingdom known as D'mt was established in Tigray. After the fall of D'mt in the 4th century BCE, Ethiopia became dominated by smaller kingdoms, like the Kingdom of Aksum in what is now Tigray and Eritrea. A Persian writer listed Aksum together with Rome, Persia, and China as one of the four major powers of the 3rd century. An old coin from AD 324 shows that Ethiopia converted to Christianity. The first interaction between Islam and Ethiopia occurred in AD 614 when the Emperor of Aksum gave refuge to several Muslims. In 912, the Zagwe Dynasty came to power and would rule the area till the late 13th century. It would last another two centuries before Ethiopia would seek to make diplomatic contact with European powers, specifically England and Portugal. However, between 1755 and 1855, Ethiopia would experience a period of isolation during which emperors lost their power to become figureheads. In reality, the country was dominated by regional lords, sultans and noblemen. Tigray – which is still a centre of upheaval – was ruled by Ras Mikael Sehul. Isolationism would end, for a while, in 1855 when a British mission concluded an alliance between the different nations within Ethiopia. The power of the emperor was restored, and he began modernising his country and recentralising power. At the same time, Ethiopia began to take part in world affairs. Ethiopia, by then called Abyssinia, was invaded twice in 1875 and 1876 by Turkish/Egyptian forces, accompanied by European and American 'advisers'. However, the invaders were twice defeated.

Ethiopia, as we know it today, began to take form under the rule of Emperor Menelik II (1889– 1913). His armies annexed several territories, populated by Oromo, Sidama, Gurage and Welayta people, committing many atrocities during their campaigns. It is estimated the number of people killed during these conquests grew into the millions. In the early 20th century, Emperor Haile Selassie Ras Tafari became the president of the country. As he and his parents had ethnic links to three of Ethiopia's largest ethnic groups (Oromo, Amhara and Gurage), he managed to unite many of the people living in his country. The independence of Ethiopia was endangered by the Italo–Ethiopian War, which started with the invasion of the country by troops of fascist Italy in 1935. They occupied the country until 1941. Mussolini proclaimed Ethiopia as an Italian territory of King Vittorio Emanuele III, who took the title of Emperor of the country. Although Ethiopia was never colonised in the real sense of the word, the Italians made large investments in the country. The development of the infrastructure became a priority, including the construction of roads and railways. The Italian government also abolished slavery, a practice that had existed in the country for centuries. During the East African Campaign in 1941, British forces – assisted by Ethiopian resistance soldiers – liberated the country, although guerrilla warfare with Italian soldiers would continue until 1943.

In 1952, Haile Selassie tried to establish a federation with Eritrea, but he had to dissolve it again in 1962 when he annexed Eritrea, leading to the Eritrean War of Independence. The worldwide oil crisis in 1973, which caused a sharp increase in gasoline prices, motivated taxi drivers and teachers to go on strike on 18 February 1974; students and workers would follow. Discontent among the middle class, created through modernisation, spread. Food shortages, famine, diseases, and border wars would result. On 20 February 1974, the feudal oligarchical cabinet of Aklilu Habte-Wold was toppled, and a new government was formed with Endelkachew Makonnen as prime minster. Haile Selassie himself would be deposed some months later. A new Provisional Military Administrative Council was established by the Derg, a Soviet-backed Marxist–Leninist military dictatorship. Several coups, uprisings and strikes would result. Political unrest, combined with wide-scale drought and a huge refugee problem, made Ethiopia into one of the poorest countries in Africa. In 1977, Somalia invaded Ethiopia during the Ogaden War. After receiving massive military aid from the USSR, Cuba, South Yemen, East Germany and North Korea, Ethiopia recovered, but peace did not fully return. In 1977–78, thousands of people were killed as a result of 'Red Terror', a response by the government to what it called 'White Terror'– a chain of violent events and assassinations by 'petty bourgeois reactionaries'. Insurrections against communist rule started in 1983–85, during a new period of famine that affected about eight million people and killed at least one million of them. This insurrection took place at a moment when the Soviet Union, under Mikhail Gorbachev, began to retreat from building world communism. In 1991, a new Transitional Government of Ethiopia with a Council of Representatives was established, and, three years later, a new constitution was written. Since then, the governments of Ethiopia managed to partly restore peace. Thanks to substantial Chinese aid, the country was able to tackle its problems and modernise.

Modern Ethiopia has a population of about 110 million people, who speak nearly 90 different languages, although English is the most popular foreign language amongst the younger population. Ethiopian Orthodox, Islam and Protestantism are the most important religions. The country has now returned to 'normality', so its very rich cultural heritage can attract thousands of visitors every year. Ethiopian Airlines, established in 1946, obviously had to cope with the many political and economic problems of its home country. Looking back to its first days in 1946, it is hard to imagine Ethiopian becoming a healthy airline that acts as the African aviation powerhouse today and the soon-to-be architect of aviation in the whole African continent.

When writing this book, I consulted several sources, newspapers and magazines relating to the story of Ethiopia and its airline. But I would especially like to thank all the people who offered insight and information enabling me to evaluate the many publications I had consulted. And of course, it would not have been possible to publish this book without the help of so many photographers worldwide who offered their best pictures to illustrate this book. Further thanks goes to Key Publishing, for allowing me to tell this story, and to my wife's patience while I was collecting and studying information and finally writing this book.

A Boeing 787 Dreamliner. (Ethiopian Airlines)

Chapter 1
Early Days of Aviation

With the introduction of aviation and the start-up of national carrier Ethiopian Airlines, Ethiopia could open up to the rest of the world. The introduction of aviation in the African country was, however, rather slow, as both Empress Zewditu and the minister of war were rather conservative and opposed to modern technology. However, the reality of Italian fascist plans of conquest in Africa forced the Ethiopian government to consider setting up a small air force. In 1929, it was decided to purchase a limited number of aircraft from Europe. An order for two aircraft was placed in Germany, but the delivery was delayed. The aircraft were transported by a steamer owned by the Norddeutscher Lloyd to the Port of Djibouti. However, when local workers saw that the French steamer SS *Porthos* was also arriving and bringing a French aircraft, they decided to assist the French in arriving in Ethiopia first by putting all kinds of difficulties in the way of the Germans. Therefore, it was a French aircraft that disembarked first in Ethiopia. With the arrival of the Potez 25, piloted by André Maillet on 18 August 1929, a new age in communication and transportation began. A few weeks after Maillet's arrival, the first Junkers aircraft arrived, piloted by Baron von Engel, who would organise the first airmail services. Maillet set up a flying school and, soon, other French pilots and mechanics arrived in Ethiopia, while Maillet and von Engel were busy transporting money, mail and people from Addis Ababa to the surrounding provinces.

It was foreign pilots who first brought aviation to Ethiopia. However, it was not long before Ethiopian pilots would earn their wings. Mishka Babicheff (who was half-Russian and half-Ethiopian) and Asfaw Ali received training in France, followed by on-site training in the flying school of André Maillet.[1] Babicheff, subsequently, became chief pilot of the Ethiopian Air Force, which was based at Jan Hoy Meda, not far from the Menelik Palace. Slowly but surely, the number of indigenous pilots began to grow. By 1935, the Ethiopian fleet consisted of 15 aircraft of different types. A small, redesigned Junkers monoplane, which was assembled in the country, was the most remarkable plane in the fleet. It had been designed by a German pilot, Ludwig Weber, who also supervised the construction and made the first test flights. The plane, designed for flights at higher altitudes, was named *Tsehai* after Emperor Haile Selassie's daughter; later the name was changed to *Ethiopia I*. In addition, several new airfields became available. In 1931, only two years after the arrival of Maillet, Ethiopia already counted eight airfields, with varying degrees of support services.

Because of the Italian colonial expansionism in Africa, Haile Selassie called for Western aviation experts and technicians to aid his country by strengthening the Imperial Ethiopian Air Force. The crisis was severe, as Italian dictator Benito Mussolini was about to invade Ethiopia with a modern army. A black American pilot by the name of John Charles Robinson – who had developed a strong affinity and respect for Africa's only independent black nation – eagerly answered this call. Robinson, who was born in Florida, had moved to Tuskegee, Alabama, with his parents.[2] After attending the Tuskegee Institute (the only institution of higher learning in Tuskegee open to black students at that time), he moved to Chicago (then a primary centre for black aviation). He managed to gain permission to follow courses at the Curtiss-Wright Aeronautical School of Chicago, which at that time was one of the leading aviation schools in the USA. He graduated at the top of his class in May 1931. Once graduated, he spent time and energy generating an interest in aviation among a new generation of African Americans, especially those of the impoverished Chicago South Side. In the fall of 1931, Robinson had become the first black instructor at the Curtiss-Wright Aeronautical School. Robinson was not content to just lay ambitious plans for uplifting future generations of African Americans, however.[3] He wanted to achieve more but realised there was no place for black Americans in the American Air Force. So, when Haile Selassie asked for foreign assistance, Robinson left for Africa in 1935. Robinson's arrival was important for the emperor's vision to train a large number of Ethiopian pilots to defend their homeland. With the assistance of an interpreter, Robinson immediately began training young Ethiopians. When Robinson's value and leadership abilities became obvious to the emperor, he gained the rank of colonel, in command of the entire Imperial Ethiopian Air Force. He trained roughly 70 pilots and even found the time to modify some aircraft to drop bombs. Because of his actions, Robinson soon earned international renown as the 'Brown Condor of Ethiopia'.

In 1934, Switzerland also contributed to Ethiopia's aviation scene. Photographer and filmmaker Walter Mittelholzer, who was also one of the co-founders of Swissair, organised an expedition by plane to Palestine and Ethiopia to deliver three Fokker three-engined aircraft to the emperor. His crews started from Zürich and flew via Port Said, Jerusalem, Tel Aviv, Petra, Ma'an, Aswan and Kassala to Addis Ababa in 46 hours and 28 minutes. The expedition lasted from 2 February until 23 February 1934.

Just as aviation in Ethiopia was beginning to pick up steam, the dark clouds of World War Two appeared on the horizon. Whereas, in general, historians consider the Anschluss of Austria in 1938 or the annexation of the Sudetenland (also in 1938) as the start of the war, some others point at the invasion of Poland by Nazi troops. However, in 1935, there were already signs of the expansionist policy that characterised the Axis powers and the ineffectiveness of the League of Nations before the outbreak of the war. Actually, the Italo-Ethiopian War could be seen as a sign of the failure of the League of Nations. On 3 October 1935, Marshal Emilio De Bono attacked Ethiopia from Italy's colonial possession in Eritrea with an army of two hundred thousand soldiers. At the same time, General

Before the start of World War Two, the Ethiopian Emperial Air Forces had obtained a few different types of aircraft, like this Junkers W 33. (Walter Mittelholzer, ETH-Bibliothek Zürich, public domain)

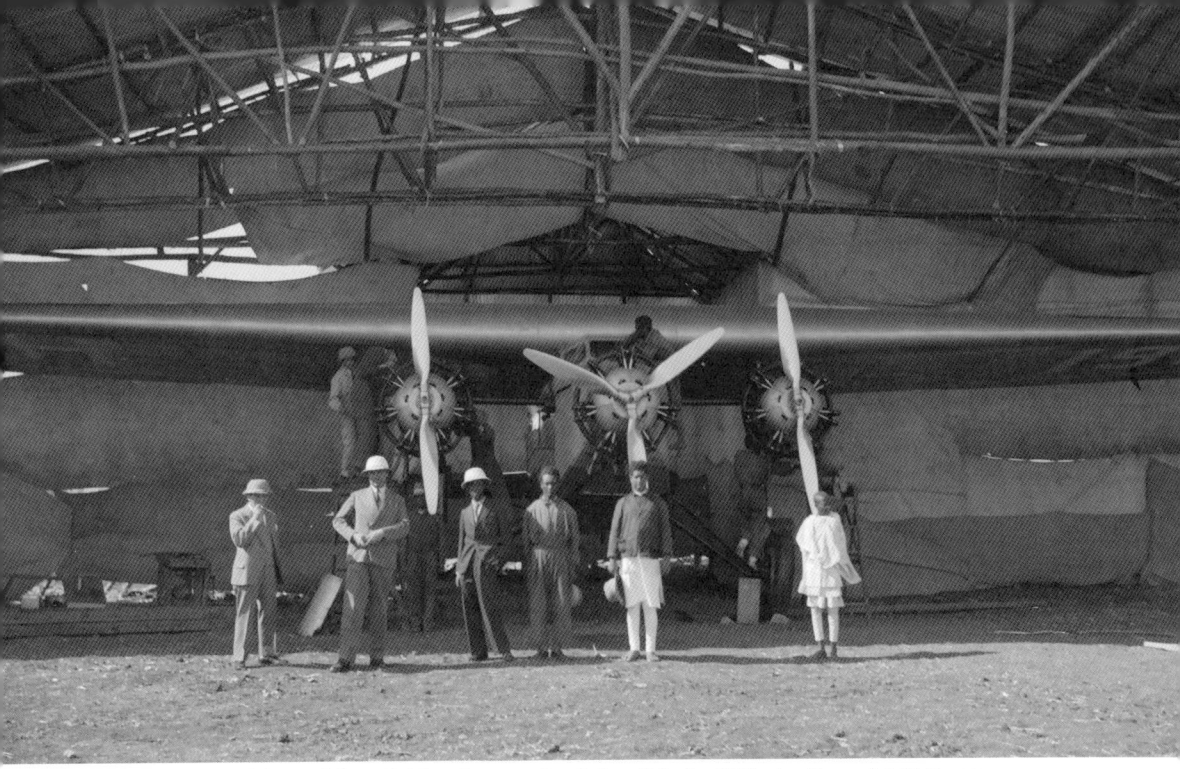

Walter Mittelholzer delivered three Fokker three-engined aircraft to the Ethiopian Emperial Air Force. (Walter Mittelholzer, ETH-Bibliothek Zürich, public domain)

Rodolfo Graziani's forces attacked from Italian Somalia. A formal declaration of war had not been delivered prior to this invasion. On 15 October, Italian troops seized Aksum.[4] An obelisk adorning the city was taken to Rome to be placed as a symbol of victory in front of the building of the Ministry of Colonies, created by the fascist regime. When Ethiopian troops were defeated and its air force mostly destroyed, Italy announced the annexation of the territory of Ethiopia, and Italian King Vittorio Emanuele III was proclaimed emperor. The provinces of Eritrea, Italian Somaliland, and Abyssinia (Ethiopia), which were occupied by Italian troops, were united to form the Italian province of East Africa. During the conflict, war crimes were committed by both sides. Italian troops used mustard gas in aerial bombardments and deliberately attacked ambulances and hospitals. The European powers – guided by Britain and France – preferred Italy as an ally against Germany, so they did not take steps to discourage the Italian invasion. Besides, the Italian fascist government and Britain had already signed a secret pact in December 1925, aimed at reinforcing Italian dominance in the region. According to this pact, London recognised that the area of high Ethiopia was an Italian zone of interest. Furthermore, a Franco–Italian agreement was signed on 7 January 1935, which gave Italy a free hand in Africa in return for Italian co-operation against Hitler. Furious about Italy's pact with France, Hitler decided to send arms to the Ethiopian forces.

Some 50 foreign mercenaries had joined the Ethiopian forces, including French pilot Pierre Corriger and Trinidadian pilot Hubert Julian, alongside a team of Belgian fascists and Cuban mercenaries. In the meantime, fighting between Italian and Ethiopian forces continued until February 1937. It would take until 1939 before rebel activities were suppressed by the Italians. Finally, in September 1943, an armistice was signed between Italy and Ethiopia. In 1944, Ethiopia was liberated by Allied forces. The treaty signed in Paris by the Italian Republic and the Allied powers of World War Two on 10 February 1947 included the formal Italian recognition of Ethiopian independence. If the Italian invasion of Ethiopia had left one positive result, it was certainly the fact that during the occupation, the first regular passenger flights were organised between Ethiopia and Europe. It was

A mail plane as used by the African American pilot Robinson during his stay in Ethiopia. (Ethiopian Air Force, photographer unknown, public domain)

the Italian airline – Ala Littoria – that started twice-weekly flights between Addis Ababa and Rome. In the meantime, in 1944, Robinson had returned to Ethiopia and established, again, a pilot training school sponsored by his friend Prince Makonnen Haile Selassie, the emperor's second son. Together with Prince Makonnen, Robinson also set up Sultan Airways Ltd. This venture would lead to the establishment of Ethiopian Airlines.

Above: Although Ethiopian ambulance aircraft clearly displayed red cross signs, they were destroyed by Italian forces during the invasion. (Ethiopian Air Force/Smithsonian Institute, photographer unknown, public domain)

Left: An Ethiopian Air Force scout plane as used by the African American pilot Robinson during his stay in Ethiopia. (Ethiopian Air Force/Smithsonian Institute, photographer unknown, public domain)

Right: When Walter Mittelholzer delivered three Fokker aircraft to the Emperor of Ethiopia, the airport in Addis Ababa was still under construction. (Walter Mittelholzer, ETH-Bibliothek, Zürich, public domain)

Below: One of Mittelholzer's Fokker aircraft in front of the Addis Ababa airport building under construction. (Walter Mittelholzer, ETH-Bibliothek, Zürich, public domain)

Chapter 2

Start Up with American Help

In the early 1940s, Emperor Haile Selassie intended to create a national airline to change the country's poverty-stricken image. In 1944, Ethiopia had already participated in the Chicago Conference, and it became one of the first African countries to sign the Convention of the International Civil Aviation Organization. The same year, the Ethiopian Civil Aviation Authority was established to handle economic and technical regulations, airport services and aviation security. Ethiopia did not have the financial or human resources to set up an airline, but the vision of the country's leadership resulted, nonetheless, in the birth of the airline in 1946. The conclusion of World War Two offered the opportunity to establish a civilian airline. Ethiopia dispatched a delegation to the founding conference of the United Nations to seek assistance from the United States. It was the US Department of State that arranged a meeting between this delegation and T B Wilson – then chairman of Trans World Airlines (TWA) – who agreed to assist, provided the airline came up with the capital to start up operations. Of course, TWA was convinced that Ethiopia could become an important hub in the region, given the strategic location of the country near the Red Sea. At the same time, the Ethiopian delegation also negotiated with Swedish carrier ABA, but these negotiations would ultimately remain unproductive.

In September 1945, TWA agreed to provide technical management and operational services, whereas business management was to be provided by a board of directors, appointed by the Ethiopian government, as well as TWA officials. Furthermore, TWA would also select potential employees and train them in aircraft maintenance and repair. In exchange, the American airline would obtain a fixed payment, based on revenue. The agreement was signed between the American airline and John H Spencer, the foreign affairs adviser to Ethiopia. The airline started its existence with a capital of 2.5m Ethiopian birr (ETB), divided into 25,000 shares that were entirely held by the Ethiopian government. The first Ethiopian Air Lines (EAL) chairman of the board of directors and president of the airline was the minister of communications, Fitawrari Tafesse Habtemichael, whereas H M Holloway was appointed as the first general manager. The official charter, which was signed several months later, was also the beginning of EAL. The charter did not only allow EAL to provide air services, but gave it the power to issue airworthiness certificates to aircraft registered in Ethiopia.[1] One can suppose that African-American pilot Robinson, who had earlier helped in setting up the Ethiopian Air Force, had been instrumental in the negotiations between TWA and the Ethiopian government.

As the airline now needed a fleet to start up operations, EAL's general manager, H M 'Dutch' Holloway, went to Egypt, where the airline purchased five surplus C-47 (DC-3) aircraft from the American forces. He also managed to recruit five American pilots able to fly these aircraft. The aircraft arrived in Addis Ababa on 1 February 1946, loaded with spare parts and accompanied by a sixth aircraft, which transported the crews back to Cairo. A week later, the airline flew its first charter operation to Nairobi, which carried a shipment of East African currency on behalf of the Ethiopian State Bank.[2]

To convince an often-sceptical public, the airline initially offered scenic flights over Addis Ababa. Regular scheduled passenger services were set up shortly afterwards, starting with domestic routes.

Following the successful inaugural flight to Cairo, a weekly service was established. Weekly services to Djibouti and Aden followed, as well as a domestic flight to Jimma. As demand for additional services increased, four more C-47 Skytrains were purchased towards the end of 1946. These ex-US military aircraft offered little comfort. They all had folding bench-type canvas seats along the sides in a military layout, and cargo was transported in the central aisle.³ Loads of coffee, honey or hides were lashed to the floor. By the time the aircraft arrived in Ethiopia in 1946, Holloway had been replaced by Henry Bruce Obermiller as general manager, who was replaced a year later by Waldon Gene Golien.

Right: The crew that made the first international flight from Addis Ababa to Cairo. (Agence Nationale de l'Aviation Civile du Gabon, photographer unknown, public domain)

Below: Douglas DC-3 and C-47 aircraft would serve Ethiopian for nearly 40 years. (Ethiopian Airlines)

Ethiopian Dakotas served some 21 domestic destinations. (Ethiopian Airlines)

Although the aircraft were not very comfortable, they enabled EAL to start up several new routes, such as Addis Ababa–Khartoum and Addis Ababa–Nairobi. In 1947, three more Dakotas were purchased. This time, the former Swissair aircraft had 21 converted forward-facing seats, increasing passenger comfort. That year, a route to Mukalla was inaugurated, followed by routes to Port Sudan, Lydda (now Lod International Airport in Israel) and Bombay (now Mumbai). The route to Bombay was operated in co-operation with BOAC. While EAL was flying as far as Aden, BOAC operated the

Ethiopian Airlines bought three Dakotas with forward-facing seats from Swissair. This aircraft is seen at Zürich Kloten Airport prior to delivery. (ETH-Bibliothek, Zürich, Bildarchiv Stiftung Luftbild Schweiz)

Aden–Bombay leg (the service to India would be stopped in 1953). In the late 1940s, EAL started charter flights to Jeddah to answer the demand of Ethiopian Muslims, wishing to perform their pilgrimages. The domestic network was also expanded as more airstrips were opened. In 1949, the airline made profit of £40,000, and a year later, a total number of 22,782 passengers were transported, compared to 19,925 the year before. According to a news report in the British magazine *Flight*, published on 4 May 1951, aircraft miles flown rose from 1,265,530 in 1949 to 1,305,725 a year later. The same year, regular flights to Karachi, Jeddah, Dhahran, and Sharjah were introduced. The flight to Sharjah was discontinued in 1953.

While the Douglas DC-3 Skytrain would remain in service on domestic routes for some 40 years, the aircraft quickly became outdated for international services. Ethiopian bought two Convair 240s in 1950, followed by a third one (bought from Belgian carrier Sabena) in 1955. These deals were financed through a US$1m loan from the American EXIM Bank. With fully finished interiors (including 36 seats), these pressurised aircraft could fly higher in smoother air, but they needed a longer runway. In the beginning, jet-assisted take-off (JATO) canisters were used during take-off from some shorter runways, as well as from the Addis Ababa airport with an elevation of 8,000ft above sea level. They remained in service until a misaligned canister blew a hole into an airframe on take-off.[4] Thankfully, the pilots were able to make an emergency landing without injury to the passengers. Needless to say, this was the last time JATO canisters were used.

Despite the new aircraft, Ethiopian Airlines encountered both political and economic competition, slowing down the expansion of the airline. International destinations like Khartoum and Nairobi were located within British colonies. Not too keen to expand competition in their backyard, EAL was often denied landing rights by the British authorities in those places. And, in rare cases, when EAL was allowed to land, it was often in less threatening secondary airfields miles away from the intended destination. Competition was also harsh, as EAL had to face other airlines that operated superior aircraft. In the end, Ethiopian saw the need to buy larger and more appealing aircraft, such as the Douglas DC-6B Cloudmaster. On the other hand, TWA seemed to favour EAL, as it appointed the airline as its general sales agent in Kenya, Tanganyika, Uganda, and Zanzibar.[5]

In 1953, EAL re-negotiated the contract with TWA to eventually change the personnel entirely to Ethiopians. The national Airline Training Project was set up, with assistance from the American government, to train local pilots, technicians, and supervisory personnel in preparation for this transition. In January 1957, Captain Alemayehu Abebe was appointed as the first Ethiopian Airlines aircraft commander. In the meantime, the airline had established its own maintenance facility in Addis Ababa, reducing the need for maintenance overseas. In 1957, EAL started long-haul flights to Frankfurt. To support the Addis Ababa–Cairo–Athens–Frankfurt route, two Douglas DC-6B Cloudmasters with 71 seats had been ordered in 1956, with an option on one more aircraft of the same type. These aircraft entered the fleet in 1958. This deal was also financed through the EXIM Bank. Crews were trained by Swissair in Zürich. The aircraft were also used on the routes to Liberia and Accra and, briefly, on a flight to Benghazi (from 7 November 1956 until 15 January 1957). As the Cloudmasters required a long runway, the decision was made to build an entirely new airport and headquarters at Bole.[6] While the DC-6Bs started international long-distance routes, the Convairs were redeployed to serve domestic and regional routes. Flights to two Yemeni cities, Hodeida and Taiz, started on 1 September 1957. On 4 June 1957, a Lockheed Constellation entered the fleet, but it was destroyed a few weeks later, on 10 July 1957, in an accident in Sudan. The aircraft had been given as a gift to the emperor, who declined the offer. Subsequently, Ethiopian had purchased the plane for US$1.6m. Notwithstanding the expansion of the airline, EAL entered a downward financial trend. Finally, on 1 January 1959, EAL joined International Air Transport Association (IATA).

Above: A series of Ethiopian Airlines' Dakotas at the old airport in Addis Ababa. (Ethiopian Airlines)

Left: Alemayehu Abebe was the first Ethiopian airline captain. (Ethiopian Airlines)

Ethiopian Airlines Convair loading khat in Dire Dawa, bound for Djibouti circa 1960. (By Bair175, own work, CC BY-SA 4.0, https://commons.wikimedia.org/w/index.php?curid=37848303)

Above: Ethiopian Airlines used the Convair on domestic and regional routes. (Thijs Postma collection)

Below: Ethiopian Airlines used JATO cannisters for take-offs from short runways or at high-altitude airports. (Ethiopian Airlines)

Ethiopian Airlines: The African Aviation Powerhouse

Left: A foreign crew in front of a Convair, ready for the next flight. (Ethiopian Airlines)

Below: The introduction of the DC-6B enabled Ethiopian Airlines to start up long-distance flights. (Paul Howard via Mick West)

This DC-6 was delivered to Ethiopian Airlines in 1978 and was scrapped later on. The aircraft was second hand and had served in Canada with Conair Aviation. (Richard Vandervord)

Above: This DC-6B is seen at Asmara Airport. (Dave Welsh)

Below: Ethiopian Airlines had only one Constellation in its fleet, but it was destroyed a few weeks after delivery. (Ethiopian Airlines via Twitter)

Chapter 3
The Jet Age

The early 1960s saw the introduction of jet services with many airlines. Ethiopian Air Lines obviously wanted to add such aircraft to its own fleet as well. A choice had to be made between the SE-210 Caravelle, the Comet 4 and the Boeing 720B. The hot and high conditions at some airports made the Caravelle inappropriate, whereas the Comet was considered obsolete.[1] Eventually, it was decided to purchase two Boeing 720 jets in August 1960, with delivery planned for 1961. In this way, Ethiopia became the first country in Africa to buy this type of aircraft. In the meantime, a new east–west service was inaugurated, linking Addis Ababa with Monrovia in Liberia via Khartoum and Accra. This was the first direct air link between East and West Africa operated by any airline.

Unfortunately, the delivery of the 720s had to be postponed until 1962, as the airfield in Addis Ababa was only just sufficient for aircraft like the DC-6B, and operating jets from that field was absolutely out of the question. The Ethiopian government had already approved the construction of a new airport in the Bole neighbourhood of Addis Ababa, but it would take until 3 December 1962, before the first two jets landed there. The new aircraft, purchased directly from Boeing, were given the registration ET-AAG and ET-AAH and were named *Blue Nile* and *White Nile*, respectively.

It was not only the state of the Addis Ababa airport that was cause for concern. On 1 March 1960, a DC-3 on a domestic route from Bulchi to Jimma crashed. On 5 September 1961, another DC-3 crashed shortly after take-off from Sendafa. Owing to these accidents, the Civil Aviation Department decided to investigate. It was discovered that the lack of infrastructure at many airfields had contributed to the accidents.[2] When, on 13 January 1962, another Dakota crashed shortly after take-off from the Tippi airfield, it was decided that the airfields at Mizan Teferi and Tippi should be closed.

On 15 January 1963, the 720B began its service with Ethiopian Air Lines on the route to Nairobi, and the next day, the second aircraft opened up a new route to Madrid, with stops in Asmara and Athens. Soon afterwards, Frankfurt was also added to the network. On 1 April, the 720B replaced the DC-6B on the Addis Ababa–Athens route. The same year, Ethiopian Air Lines entered into a pool agreement with Aden Airways and Sudan Airways on the Khartoum–Asmara–Aden route. On 8 May 1963, flights to Conakry were launched, whereas Kano (which had been served since 18 March 1962) was removed from the list of destinations. A third Boeing 720B aircraft arrived in 1964, enabling the airline to start up flights to Rome on a weekly base. This flight was routed via Khartoum or Athens as part of a pool agreement with Alitalia. Meanwhile, the elderly Skytrains and DC-3s continued to fly the domestic and cargo services and six further DC-3s were bought during the next decade. Despite their age, these aircraft were ideally suited to Ethiopia's difficult flying conditions.

In 1964, the airline commissioned a Pilot Training School and an Aviation Maintenance Technician School. These centres played an important role in the training of pilots and technicians, not only for the airline's own use, but for airlines from other African countries, as well as the Middle East.[3] In 1965, the company changed its legal status from a corporation to a share company. At the same time, the name was changed from Ethiopian Air Lines to Ethiopian Airlines.[4] By 1966, the relationship with TWA was adjusted to reflect the transfer of management with the appointment of an Ethiopian manager, Colonel Semret Medhane.[5] At that time, Medhane was heading the technical services of the Imperial Ethiopian Air Force, after previous roles a pilot and aeronautical engineer. In 1999, he received an African Aviation Individual Achievement Award for outstanding services to the African aviation industry. In the meantime, fleet modernisation went on and the airline ordered two Boeing 707-320Cs, the first of which was to be delivered in March 1968, and Ethiopian added two second-hand Boeing 720s to its fleet, which were purchased from Continental Airlines. Owing to the expanding Boeing fleet, Ethiopian decided to buy a Boeing 720B flight simulator, making the airline independent of foreign airlines for its pilot training. In 1975, it ordered five Dash 7 aircraft to be used on domestic and regional routes.

Ethiopian Air Lines entered the jet age with two Boeing 720Bs. (Mick West)

Ethiopian Air Lines cabin crew proudly show their uniforms in front of the new jets. (Jozef Mols collection)

Above: Boeing 707s joined the fleet of 720s. (Mick West)

Left: Ethiopian Air Lines took this publicity photo showing the new jet with 'The Lion of Abyssinia'. (Jozef Mols collection)

Below: The three-engined 727 replaced the four-engined 720 on many international routes. (Richard Vandervord)

Whereas the first half of the decade marked notable progress for Ethiopian Airlines, the tides changed in the second half. Opinion within Ethiopia turned against Haile Selassie because of the 1973 Oil Crisis, a worldwide problem. In February 1974, gasoline prices sharply increased as a result of the crisis. Taxi drivers and teachers went on strike that month, and students and workers in Addis Ababa began demonstrating against the government. The cabinet of Aklilu Habte-Wold was forced to resign and a new government was formed with Endelkachew Makonnen as prime minister.[6] Haile Selassie was deposed by the Derg, a Soviet-backed Marxist–Leninist military dictatorship led by Mengistu Haile Mariam. In March 1975, the new Provisional Military Administration Council established a one-party communist state. To make things worse, the new government suffered several coups, uprisings, wide-scale drought and a huge refugee problem. In 1977, Somalia, which had previously received assistance and aid from the Soviet Union, invaded Ethiopia in the Ogaden War, capturing the Ogaden region (a desert area in the east of Ethiopia, bordering Somalia). When Ethiopia, in turn, received aid from the Soviet Union, Cuba, South Yemen, North Korea and East Germany, it was able to recover the occupied region. In 1977–78, about 500,000 people died because of forced deportations and the use of hunger as a weapon under Mengistu's rule. The government used terror in response to the 'White Terror', a chain of violent assassinations and killings, carried out by 'bourgeois reactionaries' who wanted to reverse the revolution. Ethiopia became infamous worldwide for severe drought, famine of epic proportions and accusations that the policies of the Derg were aimed at intentionally exacerbating the situation. The country would spiral into civil war for almost 16 years, as various rebel factions attempted to oust the Derg or to break away altogether.

Of course, this situation was not favourable for tourism, one of the mainstays of the airline's success. Furthermore, the government cut back on official international travel and also limited tourism. This was harmful for Ethiopian Airlines, as it cut revenue out of the profitable international routes and cargo operations that had paid for losses on less-profitable domestic routes. Furthermore, landing fees at home increased, rising fuel prices had to be paid for and several labour revolts resulted in costlier concessions from management and greater competition from foreign airlines trying to 'eat a piece of the pie' left over by ailing Ethiopian Airlines.

As a result, the airline was forced to raise fares while cutting back on domestic operations. Four stations were closed in a single month. As the airline was trying to stay solvent, it decided to wet lease aircraft to several foreign carriers, including Saudia, Air India and Air Algérie. At the end of the '70s, and mainly thanks to government contracts, it seemed Ethiopian would return to profitability, but the airline would encounter enormous successive losses at the close of the decade. The financial situation of the carrier was so bad that suppliers were only willing to deliver fuel to its aircraft if payment was made in cash upon delivery.

Although it seemed Ethiopia was falling apart, the 1980s would mark a transition towards profitability for its national airline. At the beginning of the decade, a new general manager – Captain Mohammed Ahmed – was appointed and he started to tackle the crisis. A lot of reforms were needed, such as firing staff to rehire them later at a lower salary level. Thanks to cash injections from the government, the airline even managed to buy new ATR-42 equipment, as well as some Canadian DC-6-300 Twin Otters to be used on domestic routes. In this way, the old DC-3 fleet could be replaced. In 1979, two Boeing 727s were bought for the medium-range routes to replace the older 720s. A third one would enter the fleet in 1982, together with two de Havilland Canada DHC-5 Buffalos for short-field transport use on domestic services. At the same time, the airline ordered two new Boeing 767-200ERs to become its flagships on the Addis Ababa–Rome route. Ethiopian Airlines had been a consistent buyer of American passenger aircraft and despite the urging of government ideologies from time to time, it had ignored opportunities to buy aircraft from the Soviet Union, the country's principal patron. The millions of dollars paid for American aeroplanes made impoverished Ethiopia the third largest export market in Africa for American goods.

The Boeing 727 was introduced to replace the oldest 720s. (Rolf Warner)

Above: An ATR-42 makes a test flight prior to delivery to the airline. (Jozef Mols collection)

Below: The ATR proved itself to be very useful on short-haul domestic routes. (Jozef Mols collection)

The ATR-42 was not the right choice for Ethiopian Airlines and was soon replaced by Fokker 50s. (Richard Vandervord)

Above: The Twin Otter was used on domestic routes to remote airfields. (Raimund Stehmann)

Below: A Twin Otter undergoing maintenance at Ethiopian Airlines' maintenance facility. (Raimund Stehmann)

ETHIOPIAN AIRLINES

APRIL 1 – OCTOBER 31, 1967

RESERVATION AND TICKET OFFICES

CITY	ADDRESS	TELEPHONE
ACCRA	111 Cocoa House, Liberty Ave.,	62656
ADDIS ABABA	Reservations and Information Haile Selassie I Square (Adowa) De Gaule Square (Piazza) Africa Hall Ghion Hotel Tekle Haimanot Sq., New Market	47444 47000 13300/01 44012 44011 16503
ADEN	Bank Flat Bldg., Steamer Point King Solomon Street, Crater Khormaksar Airport	22138, 24701 52711 23738
ASMARA	Haile Selassie I Ave., 89-91	12166, 12167
ATHENS	10 Venizelou Avenue	624601
BEIRUT	Chaker & Aoueini Bldg., Riad EL Solh Square	297870/71
CAIRO	1 Kasr el Nil Street	72709
DARESSALAAM	Holland House Independence Ave., Cor. Ohio Sts	24174, 24185
DELHI	Hotel Oberoi Intercontinental	611392,619465
DJIBOUTI	Rue de Marseille	407,877
ENTEBBE (KAMPALA)	69 Kampala Road, P.O. Box 3591	54796
FRANKFURT	Kaiserstrasse 61	250077
KARACHI	Hotel Metropole, Club Road	55456
KHARTOUM	Gamhuria Ave., Abul Ela New Bldg, P.O. Box 639	77180, 70866 77597
LAGOS	34 Breadfruit St., P.O. Box 1602	26741
LONDON	TWA, 200 Piccadilly, W. 1	TRA 1234
MADRID	Torre de Madrid 10-9, Plaza de Espana	248.06.05
NAIROBI	Mansion House, Wabera Street,	26631, 26632
PARIS	TWA, 5, Rue Scribe	0734979
ROME	TWA/ETHIOPIAN 59 Via Barberini	476-754
TAIZ	Al-Akaba Street, Thabet Andulgalil & Sons Bldg., P.O. Box 402	223
U.S.A.	Any TWA Office	
GENERAL HEADQUARTERS		
ADDIS ABABA	Haile Selassie I Airport P.O. Box 1755	47300
U.S.A. OFFICES		
LOS ANGELES	1800 North Argyle Street Hollywood, California 90028	(213)463-7333
NEW YORK	51 East 42nd Street	(212)867-0095

Cable Addresses: All cities—ETHAIR
Except: Madrid— ETHAIRMAD
New York—FLYETHAIR
All TWA offices — TWAIR

Serving ASIA EUROPE MIDDLE EAST AFRICA *Coast to Coast*

Ethiopian Airlines timetable from 1967. (Alan Bushell)

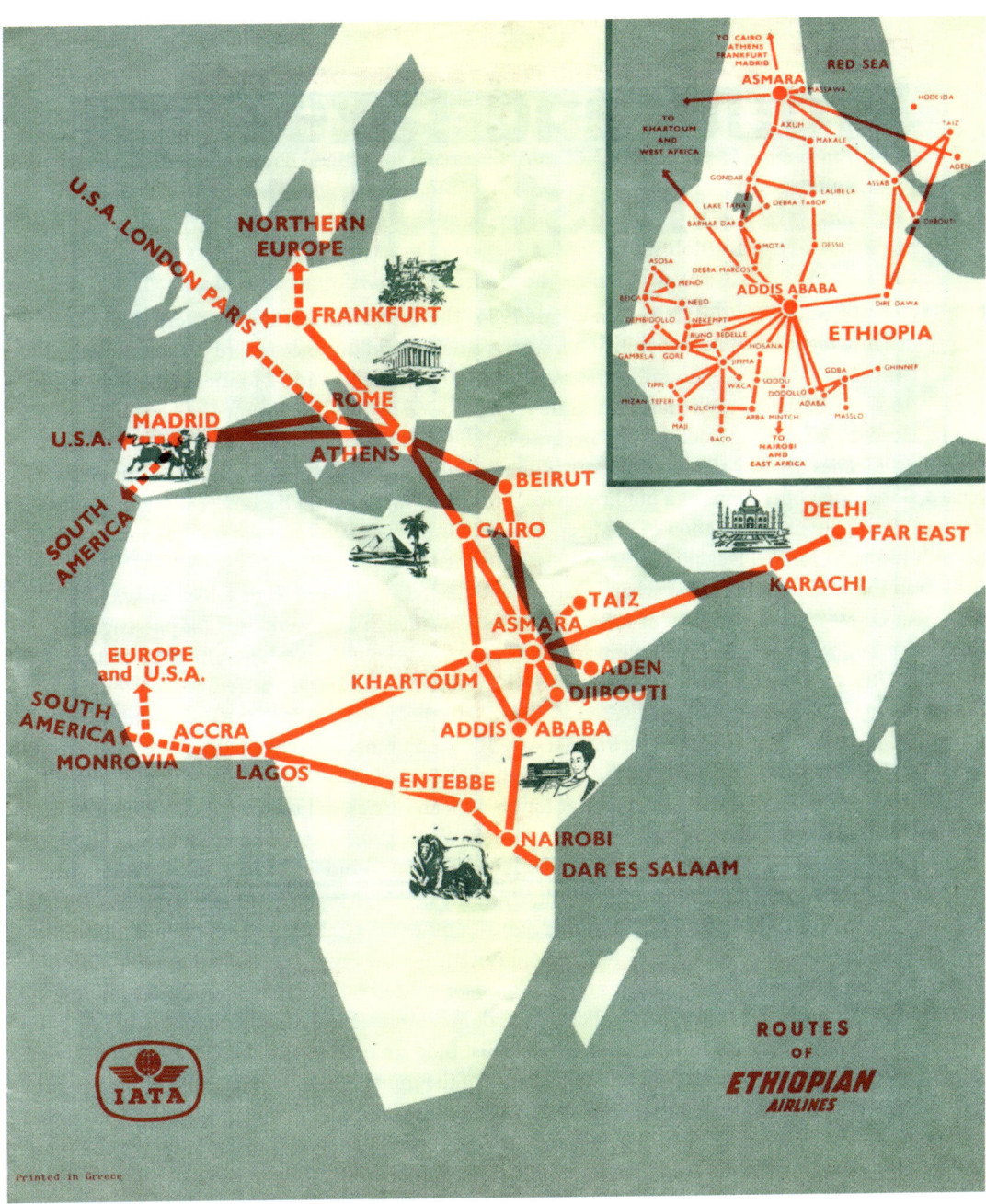

Ethiopian Airlines route map from 1967. (Alan Bushell)

did earlier, the airline also created its own frequent flyer programme, named 'Sheba Miles' after the legendary Queen of Sheba. To guarantee training for its pilots (and pilots from other African countries as well), Ethiopian installed a new state-of-the-art flight simulator for the Boeing 767. This simulator was also used to train crews on the 757, whose flight deck is very similar. In 1999, construction started on a new, ultra-modern terminal building at Bole International Airport in Addis Ababa to upgrade passenger services and cater for an anticipated increase in traffic.

The outbreak of war between Ethiopia and Eritrea forced the airline to suspend its flights to the Eritrean capital, Asmara. A border dispute between the two countries led to the Eritrean–Ethiopian War, which would last until June 2000, and cost the poor African countries an estimated US$1m per day. Of course, this war had a negative effect on Ethiopia's economy. Not only did it affect passenger numbers on domestic flights, but international tourists refrained from visiting the country. On the other hand, the war strengthened the position of the ruling coalition. In the meantime, the airline had also experienced its worst tragedy. Flight 961, a Boeing 767-200ER, was hijacked. The plane ran out of fuel and crashed off the Comoro Islands. Some passengers were saved by tourists on the beach, but 125 of the 175 passengers were not so lucky and died.

Above: The 767 was used on long-haul routes. (Jozef Mols collection)

Below: The 767 was not only used on European routes but on major African sectors. (Sander Zwart)

Thanks to the 767, Ethiopian Airlines could set up a global network, enabling the airline to grow. This was in contrast with other African carriers. (Jozef Mols collection)

Above: The 737-200 was introduced at nearly the same time as the 767-200 and was used mainly on regional routes. (Jozef Mols collection)

Below: The 757 was the 'little sister' of the 767 and was used on medium-range flights, but this aircraft was, nevertheless, pictured at Amsterdam Schiphol Airport. (Jozef Mols)

A 757 seen at the busy Addis Ababa airport. (Jozef Mols collection)

Above: With the 757PF, Ethiopian Airlines could expand its cargo operations. (Jozef Mols collection)

Below: 767-300ERs were obtained from 1996 onwards and would later replace the 767-200s. (Jonathan Druion)

The Lockheed Hercules was used for cargo flights to both domestic and regional airfields. (Jozef Mols collection)

Above: The de Havilland Canada Buffalo served in Ethiopian Airlines' cargo fleet. (Richard Vandervord)

Below: Leased Fokker 50s had to replace the ATR-42 on 'high and hot' routes. (Jozef Mols collection)

The Fokker 50s were leased just after the collapse of the Dutch aircraft manufacturer. (Jozef Mols collection)

Student pilots are trained with a fleet of Cessna-172 aircraft. (Raimund Stehmann)

Arrival of a crated Cessna-172 for the flying school. (Ethiopian Airlines)

The Cessnas of the flying school are maintained by the Ethiopian Airlines Technical School. (Ethiopian Airlines)

Chapter 5
Aggressive Expansion

In 2002, at the start of a new millennium, Ethiopian Airlines embarked on an aggressive expansion and fleet modernisation project. The airline added six 767-300ERs to its fleet between 2002 and 2012. At the same time, orders were placed for six 737-700s and one 737-260PF Cargo. The new 767s were scheduled to replace the older 767-200s, whereas the next generation 737s would replace the older 737-200s. To modernise its cargo operations and deliver a reliable service to its customers worldwide, the airline started an automated cargo booking system on 1 April 2005. This system enabled customers (shippers, consignees, and agents) to directly access information related to their consignment and to track the shipment from its origin to its final destination. In the meantime, on 21 January 2003, the airline opened its new and ultra-modern terminal at Bole International Airport. After renovation, the older terminal began to serve mainly domestic flights. The airline also started night operations out of Addis Ababa to complement the daytime flights in a move to achieve better fleet utilisation.

In February 2003, Girma Wake became the new CEO of Ethiopian Airlines. Girma had just signed a new contract with Gulf Air and had worked with the Arabian carrier for only two months when he received the offer of CEO at Ethiopian. However, Seyoum Mesfin, Ethiopia's foreign affairs minister, was able to convince Girma to leave Gulf Air and join Ethiopian Airlines.[1] At that time, Ethiopian carried 1.2 million passengers annually to 42 international and 16 domestic destinations with its fleet of only 12 jetliners. Girma spent most of 2004 devising a bold plan with the assistance of the locally based office of Ernst and Young. That is where a new strategic plan under the name of 'Vision 2010' was written. The aim was to increase passenger traffic to three million, revenue to US$1bn and employees to 6,000 by 2010. Immediately after Girma took office, operating revenues increased by 26 per cent to more than US$0.5bn in Fiscal Year (FY) 2004–05.

In 2005, the airline announced its plans to purchase the new Boeing 787 Dreamliner, which made Ethiopian Airlines the first carrier on the African continent to do so. Although the original delivery had been scheduled for 2008, the first Dreamliner would not arrive until mid-2012. The airline ordered a total of ten of these ultra-modern jets, with an option on five more. The order was valued at US$1.3bn.

In the meantime, Ethiopian Airlines had embarked on another remarkable project. African countries were facing great problems caused by plagues of locusts. These insects destroyed crops in the region, contributing to widespread famine. Therefore, Ethiopian Airlines had acquired the rights to build the Ag Cat under licence from the Schweitzer Aircraft Corporation in Elmira, New York, prior to the liquidation of this American manufacturer. The airline's technicians went to the company's plant to learn the techniques for building the plane. Soon, the airline was no longer able to meet local demand for this aircraft (known in Africa as the G-164B Eshet), which had become overwhelming. The result was that Ethiopian technicians could build up skills in the field of aircraft manufacturing while the airline generated some extra profits, and the farmers could benefit from this new weapon against the locusts.

In 2006, when Ethiopian celebrated its 60 years of services, the airline could proudly inaugurate its new maintenance hangar and cargo terminal. A year later, the airline received two awards from the *African Aviation Journal* and *The African Times/USA*. The first award was a recognition of excellent financial performance, passenger growth, route network expansion, fleet modernisation, inflight service, and overall customer care. The second award was for Ethiopian Airlines' achievement and continuing contribution to the uplift of Africa's profile and the quality of life for Africans everywhere.

The Boeing 737-700 replaced some older 737-200s. (Eduard Onyshchenko/Wikimedia Commons)

A year later, the airline entered into a codeshare agreement with Lufthansa that put Ethiopian in a position to offer daily flights from its hub in Addis Ababa to Lufthansa's hub in Frankfurt, with convenient onward flight connections to many other destinations around the world. In the same period, Ethiopian also entered into such an agreement with Brussels Airlines.

Right: To combat the locusts that caused famine in Africa, Ethiopian Airlines built the Ag Cat under licence to spray crops. (Raimund Stehmann)

Below: A new Dash 8-Q400 leaving Manchester Airport on its delivery flight to Ethiopia. (Alan Bushell)

With the delivery of the new Dash Q400, Ethiopian Airlines could replace its leased Fokker 50s. (Alan Bushell)

Above: The Dash Q400 became very popular with tourists, flying to historical sites like Bahir Dar, Gondar, Lalibela and Axum. (Alan Bushell)

Below: Ethiopian ordered a total of eight Q400s with an option on four more. (Sander Zwart)

The Dash Q400 can transport 78 passengers on domestic and regional flights between 1,000 and 1,850 nautical miles. (Alan Bushell)

In 2009, and continuing along the lines set forward in the 'Vision 2010', Ethiopian Airlines ordered 35 new aeroplanes direct from the manufacturers. The order included five Boeing 777-200LRs and 12 Airbus A350-900s. The order for the Airbus aircraft was signed during the 2009 Dubai Air Show, with deliveries scheduled between 2016 and 2019. This order evidenced the airline's dissatisfaction with Boeing for the delays in the delivery of the Dreamliner, although an order for ten of these aircraft was reconfirmed. The Dreamliners would be paid thanks to a credit from the EXIM Bank, which also covered the spare engines on order. Eight Bombardier Q400 regional aircraft with 78 seats (with an option for four more aircraft) were also ordered, the first of which arrived on 21 March 2010. The aircraft arrived from Canada after a refuelling stop in St John's, Canada, then a transatlantic crossing to Santa Maria, Azores, Portugal, followed by a refuelling stop in Cairo before the last leg from Egypt to Addis Ababa. The new aircraft enabled the airline to retire the leased Fokker 50s from the fleet by 2011, replacing the Fokkers on domestic and regional routes ranging from 1,000 to 1,850 nautical miles. On some flights, especially to historical sites (Bahir Dar, Gondar, Lalibela and Axum), the Bombardier aircraft would prove their value. All these investments enabled Ethiopian to operate one of the youngest fleets in Africa with better comfort and efficiency. In 2009, Ethiopian had already leased two McDonnell Douglas MD-11 freighters (one in January 2009 and the other in September). This way, Ethiopian Airlines managed to meet the increasing demand for cargo transportation. Cargo business had increased by 38.4 per cent compared to the previous year, while passenger numbers rose by 12.3 per cent to 2.8 million.

Also in 2009, Ethiopian Airlines showed, for the first time, its pan-African ambitions by signing a management contract with ASKY Airlines for a period of five years. The contract was an important move, creating an historic intra-African co-operation in the airline business aimed at helping the development of a West African hub in Lomé, Togo, for the regional and intercontinental routes.[2] Ethiopian took a 20 per cent share in the capital of ASKY, which started its operations in January 2010 with a fleet of Boeing 737s leased from Ethiopian Airlines. The Ethiopian share was later increased to 40 per cent, while other shareholders, spread over 11 African countries, included the private multinational Ecobank, the Bank for Investment and Development, and the West African Development Bank. Girma Wake made it no secret that Ethiopian was evaluating launching additional airlines in southern and northern Africa, possibly under joint-venture deals with other African carriers. In this way, Ethiopian Airlines would be in a position to expand its African presence in competition with carriers like Emirates and Qatar Airways that were fighting across the African continent to increase their market share. The bankruptcy of former multinational carrier Air Afrique in 2002 had made airline travel in Africa more difficult, with serious problems for goods and people traffic in West and Central Africa, and many carriers from the Gulf-region had tried to fill up the vacuum.

In 2010, Ethiopian Airlines signed a codeshare agreement with Scandinavian Airlines, one of the founding members of the Star Alliance, providing travellers with better connectivity and a broad range of services between Europe and Africa. On 15 December 2010, Ethiopian signed a similar agreement with Air China. The agreement strengthened Ethiopian's partnership with one of the global airlines in China, giving passengers of both carriers a wider choice of services between Asia and Africa. Under the agreement, the two carriers jointly provided 14 weekly flights on the Addis Ababa–Guangzhou and Addis Ababa–Beijing routes. Asian passengers, on the other hand, would be offered seamless connection via Addis Ababa to the vast Ethiopian network in Africa.[3] In June of the same year, Ethiopian also added Pointe-Noire, the second largest city in the Republic of Congo, to its network. By the end of the year, the airline had placed a firm order for ten Boeing 737-800 next generation aircraft in a deal worth US$767m. The first delivery was scheduled for November 2011.

During the period Girma was CEO of the airline, Ethiopian Airlines created about 1,500 new jobs, including 250 for foreigners. The profits the airline had made also allowed for significantly raised employee incomes. On average, every employee's pay increased by 167 per cent. Profits had increased from 269m birr to 1,345m birr in the same period. Ethiopian Airlines had become the second biggest airline in Africa, next only to South African Airways. By the end of 2010, Ethiopian Airlines had exceeded all the goals set in 'Vision 2010' and the company's net profit for the fiscal year amounted to US$121.4m. When Girma retired, he was succeeded by Tewolde GebreMariam, who would immediately launch his 'Vision 2025' project, which should take Ethiopian further on its growth path.

Ethiopian Airlines leased three MD 11s to supplement its cargo fleet. (Jozef Mols collection)

Above: Ethiopian Airlines established its own engine overhaul facility at Bole Airport. (Ethiopian Airlines)

Right: The engine overhaul facility handles engines for Ethiopian Airlines but also for other African carriers. (Ethiopian Airlines)

The engine overhaul facility provides jobs for people from Ethiopia but also from other African countries. (Ethiopian Airlines)

Above: Ethiopian's maintenance facility at Bole Airport. (Ethiopian Airlines)

Left: Ethiopian Airlines announced its order for Airbus A350 equipment during the Paris Air Show. (Airbus/F. Lancelot/Master Films)

Below: Ethiopian Airlines Aviation Academy welcomes students from all over Africa. (Ethiopian Airlines)

Aggressive Expansion

Above: Ethiopian Airlines Aviation Academy also prepares students for technical jobs within the Ethiopian Airlines group. (Ethiopian Airlines)

Right: Lomé-based ASKY Airlines started up with a fleet leased from Ethiopian Airlines. (Sander Zwart)

Below: Dash aircraft are also leased from Ethiopian airlines. (Sander Zwart)

Chapter 6
'Vision 2025'

With the arrival of Tewolde GebreMariam as the new CEO of Ethiopian Airlines, the ambitious 'Vision 2025' project was launched to further increase profits, adapt the airline to the 21st century and expand its presence in Africa and the world. It may have been an encouraging start for the new CEO that his airline obtained the Gold Award of the Year 2011/2012 from the African Aviation News Portal, the 2011 AFRAA Award for being consistently profitable over the years and the African Cargo Airline of the Year 2011 Award for its excellence in air-cargo handling.

Notwithstanding this excellent start, 2011 would prove to be a tough year for the global airline industry and Ethiopian Airlines. The net profit of the airline tumbled in FY2012 by 40 per cent to 732m birr (compared to 1.23bn birr the year before). Nevertheless, the number of passengers had increased by 25 per cent to 4.6 million. It was clear the fuel price hike had been a daunting challenge. For the first time, the price of fuel stayed high for a long time, remaining at US$120 per barrel for a year and a half. The European economic crisis reduced the demand for air travel and so did the economic growth in China and other Asian countries, which had stalled. Kenya Airways and Royal Air Maroc even had to reduce their staff; South African Airways remained in the red. And yet, Ethiopian Airlines remained profitable and was even able to make an annual salary increment of 6 to 8 per cent. This was, in part, the result of Ethiopia's double-digits economic growth and its strategic location. If a line was drawn through China, Africa, India and Brazil, Ethiopia would be right in the middle. Furthermore, it would have been unfair to compare net results of the previous year (2010–11) with the results in 2011–12, as the previous year's results had been inflated by the 20 per cent devaluation of the Ethiopian currency against the dollar in September 2010.

In January 2010, Ethiopian announced that the carrier placed orders for ten Boeing 737-800s. Some of these aircraft would be leased to ASKY Airlines, which, at that time, used a pair of older 737s, also on lease from Ethiopian. The same year, Ethiopian was the first African launch carrier for the Boeing 777-200LR passenger plane. In June 2011, the airline signed a lease with General Electric's GECAS division for two Boeing 777F aircraft on a dry lease for a period of ten years. These aircraft replaced the carrier's two 757-200 converted freighters. A few months later, Ethiopian Airlines and Boeing announced an order for four 777 freighters – an order valued at US$1.1bn. These new aircraft would significantly enhance the tonnage and range capabilities of the airline. In July 2012, an additional 777-200LR was ordered. The performance and range of the aeroplane would enable the airline to open direct routes from Washington DC to Addis Ababa and from Ethiopia to Beijing, Toronto and other long-range routes. In the meantime, Ethiopian also signed codeshare agreements with Singapore Airlines and Asiana Airlines.

To modernise its pilot training facilities, Ethiopian Airlines took delivery of four Diamond DA40NG aircraft. These aircraft were flown over in four days by Diamond pilots Thomas Bolt, Othmar Nentwich, Christian Husek and Ingmar Mayerbuch. Each was accompanied and supported by an Ethiopian Airlines pilot. The flight took them from Wiener Neustadt in Austria via Thessaloniki and Heraklion to Luxor in Egypt and Khartoum in Sudan to Addis Ababa. These four aircraft were the first of a batch of ten and one simulator to be delivered. Ethiopian Airlines made it clear it had the intention to quadruple its Ethiopian Aviation Academy annual student intake by 2025, as part of the 'Vision 2025' strategic plan. From an annual intake capacity of a little over 200 trainees a few years earlier, by 2013 this capacity had risen to over 1,000.

After being invited as a member of the Star Alliance in late 2010, the airline joined the Alliance on 13 December 2011. Ethiopian became the Alliance's third carrier based on the African continent.

'Vision 2025'

At the same time, it was also the largest and most important player within the Alliance to operate from an African hub.

On 14 August 2012, Ethiopian Airlines took delivery of its first 787-800 Dreamliner, dubbed *Africa First*. The airline was the first carrier in the world, outside Japan, and ahead of any airline in the Americas, Europe and the Middle East, to operate this type of aircraft. A second aircraft of the same type was delivered on 3 October that year. When the first Dreamliners arrived, Ethiopian Airlines decided to continue using the brand-new aircraft on rotating African destinations, to show its commitment to continue serving as the flagship carrier of Africa. This way, the fastest growing airline in Africa was enabling passengers from African destinations to enjoy first, ahead of other regions, the travel experience on board this new Boeing. Rotating destinations served by the first Dreamliner included Lagos, Johannesburg, Abuja, Malabo, Douala, Lomé, Accra, Maputo and Luanda. A few months after the arrival of the Dreamliner, on 1 November 2012, the International Lease Finance Corporation announced that Ethiopian Airlines had agreed to lease three 787-800 Dreamliners. With this order, the 787 fleet would grow in the following years from ten to 13 aircraft. The newly leased aircraft were scheduled to be delivered in the first half of 2015. Unfortunately, the introduction of the new 787-800 was not without problems. On 16 January 2013, Boeing had its most advanced aircraft grounded worldwide because of fires that started in the aeroplane's batteries. The lithium-ion technology installed on the 787 was a new feature in commercial aircraft, introduced to save weight. Several previous delays had already affected the introduction of Dreamliners. As a result, Ethiopian saw its newest aircraft grounded until mid-June 2013.

On 22 April 2013, the airline leased two 777-300ER aircraft for 12 years from the Air Lease Corporation. These aircraft were scheduled for delivery in May and June 2015.

Also in 2012, Ethiopian Airlines once again received several important awards. Its CEO won the African Business Leader of the Year Award from the Corporate Council on Africa. The airline itself received the International Diamond Prize for Excellence in Quality from the European Society for Quality Research. Furthermore, it won the African Airline of the Year Award, and Captain Desta Zeru, vice president of flight operations, obtained the Africa Legend of Travel Award from *African Travel Quarterly* magazine. The airline also received the Award for Excellent Customer Service by Planet Africa Network.

This Boeing 777-200LR was delivered in July 2013. (Yiran)

Left: Soon after the arrival of the 777-200s, the 777-300s also joined the fleet. (Severin Hackenberger)

Below: The 777-300 became the largest plane in the Ethiopian fleet. (Jackson Zeng)

The business-class cabin of the 777 provides perfect comfort for the airline's long-haul passengers. (Jozef Mols collection)

The introduction of 777 freighters dramatically increased the cargo capacity of the airline. (Severin Hackenberger)

To celebrate Ethiopian's membership of the Star Alliance, this 737-300ER received a special logo. (Sander Zwart)

As a result of the fleet expansion, the airline would increase its global footprint, rapidly growing its network. In Africa, the airline added flights to Blantyre in Malawi and Ndola in Zambia on 31 March 2013, increasing its African network to 45 destinations, including 16 domestic points. These flights were operated by 737-700 equipment, except for flights to Malawi, which were operated by 737-800. On certain routes, frequencies were also increased. In Asia, the airline added flights to Ho Chi Minh City, Manila, and Seoul Incheon in June 2013, operating from Ethiopian's existing hubs in Hong Kong and Bangkok. On these Asian routes, 767-300ER aircraft were used. South Korea is a significant provider of aid throughout Africa, funding the development of agriculture, infrastructure, technology centres and hospitals. Between 2010 and 2014, the country committed US$1.09bn in funding for infrastructure development in Africa. Bilateral trade between Vietnam and Africa, on the other hand, more than doubled between 2009 and 2011, in part because of Vietnamese investment in African energy and mining projects. Both countries were, therefore, interesting destinations for Ethiopian, hoping to generate growing business traffic on these flights.

On 1 July 2013, the airline also added São Paulo and Rio de Janeiro to its route map. These flights operated through the Ethiopian second hub in Lomé, Togo, with three flights a week using the new 787 Dreamliner. These flights were the only direct connection between West Africa and Brazil. Furthermore, Ethiopian and its partner airline, ASKY, would co-ordinate their schedules to give short, seamless, and convenient connections to West African travellers between West Africa and Brazil. This way, Ethiopia (the fastest growing economy in Africa) would be connected with the fifth largest and fastest growing economy in the world, São Paulo. On 2 July 2013, Ethiopian received its sixth 777-200LR, and on 7 November 2013 the airline also received the first of its four 777-300ERs with 400 passenger seating capacity. This aircraft would be operated on dense routes such as Guangzhou, Dubai, Luanda and Washington DC. It was clear that Ethiopian Airlines was taking advantage of some natural transfer synergies that would link the three regions to further develop Addis Ababa into a Dubai-style hub of Africa.

In the meantime, the Ethiopian Airlines maintenance facility had joined a worldwide network of facilities authorised to work on Bombardier commercial and business aircraft. Earlier, when the production under licence of the Ag Cat had come to an end, Ethiopian had announced agreements with Boeing to start up – and later expand – wire-harness production at the Wire Harness Facility in Addis Ababa. The plant had opened in 2009 and started supplying seat-to-seat wire harnesses for all Boeing commercial aeroplane programmes.

In the same period, Ethiopian Airlines further implemented its pan-African ambitions. In February 2013, the airline was selected by Malawi's Public Private Partnership Commission as the preferred bidder to become a strategic partner of the failed state-owned national carrier Air Malawi. The airline could acquire a stake of up to 49 per cent in the privatised airline, with Malawi's government holding a 20 per cent share and the remainder being offered to private investors in Malawi. Landlocked Malawi is one of Africa's most densely populated and least developed countries. Air Malawi had been placed in voluntary liquidation by the government in November 2012, after two failed restructuring projects.[1] At that time, its debts amounted to about US$50m. The assets of the airline had been transferred to a new company under the same name, and the airline continued its operations, while the government was seeking to complete an equity partnership to recapitalise the airline. Air Malawi operated limited services on a network of five domestic and regional routes, including Lilongwe, Johannesburg, Harare, and Lusaka. As the carrier's subsidiary, Air Cargo was apparently profitable, operating airfreight services between Malawi, Europe and the Far East; this division was separated from the privatised company and, therefore, not included in the equity sale. On 11 July 2013, the shareholder agreement between Ethiopian and the government of Malawi was signed. To further expand its African footprint, Ethiopian Airlines and RwandAir signed a technical support agreement on 18 December 2013. As per the agreement, Ethiopian would provide technical support services to RwandAir as of March 2014 for line maintenance up to a check and component exchange support for Boeing 737NG and Bombardier Q400 aircraft. The Ethiopian MRO Services would then deploy a technical team in Kigali to carry out the day-to-day activities on site, while being supported as required from the main base in Addis Ababa.

By the end of FY2013, Ethiopian Airlines could once again show positive results. The airline had handled 5.2 million passengers and that was a new record that represented a 12 per cent increase compared with 2012. Even though the load factor went down by 0.6 per cent, the financial year showed that total revenue was up by 9.2 per cent to US$2.15bn. According to the IATA annual airlines ranking, Ethiopian was the first in Africa and the 37th in the world in terms of revenue, as well as the number one in Africa and the 18th in the world in operating profit. This historical ranking achieved by the airline was a testimony of the soundness of its 'Vision 2025' strategic roadmap. The good results were obtained in spite of the 787 grounding that affected operations for six months, combined with the cancellation of night Harare–Lusaka flights.

Above: This Cessna 206 served for several years in the Ethiopian Airlines Aviation Academy prior to the arrival of new Diamond DA40 aircraft. (Raimund Stehmann)

Right: The Ethiopian Airlines Aviation Academy also used the Piper PA-34-200T Seneca. (Raimund Stehmann)

Below: The Ethiopian Airlines Aviation Academy also used the Piper PA-34-200T Seneca. (Raimund Stehmann)

Ethiopian Airlines ordered a total of ten aircraft for its training activities. (Diamond Aircraft)

Above: Delivery of four Diamond aircraft for the Ethiopian Airlines Aviation Academy. (Diamond Aircraft)

Below: This 737-400F was leased in September 2013 from Aviation Capital Group and was destroyed on 10 January 2015 when, on a flight from Lomé to Accra, the airplane overran the runway upon landing. (Sander Zwart)

Boeing 737-700s were used on regional routes to African countries. (Sander Zwart)

Above: 737-800 equipment was mainly used on medium-haul routes in Africa. (Sander Zwart)

Below: A 737-800 in Cotonou. This aircraft was later transferred to ASKY, a subsidiary of Ethiopian Airlines. (Sander Zwart)

A 737-800 seen at the Bole International Airport in Addis Ababa. (Alan Wilson, Wikimedia Commons licence)

Ethiopian Airlines took a minority participation in the new Malawian airline, which receives some of Ethiopian's aircraft on lease. (Wesley Moolman)

Above: Ethiopian Airlines made some Boeing 737 jets available to its partner airline Malawian. (Jacobus Saayman)

Right: An Ethiopian 737 operating for Malawian. (Steve Brimley)

Below: Ethiopian provides line maintenance for RwandAir's Boeing fleet. (Sander Zwart)

Chapter 7

Pan-African Vision Pays Off

As a result of its 'Vision 2025' strategic plan and its pan-African ambitions, Ethiopian Airlines was ranked as the largest carrier in Africa for revenue and profit, according to IATA.[1] The airline operated the youngest fleet in the continent, with an average of less than seven years, and it was serving 84 international destinations across five continents with over 200 daily departures. During FY2013–14, capacity measured in available seat kilometres (ASK) grew by 17.2 per cent, whereas revenue passenger kilometres (RSK) increased by 16 per cent; passenger numbers were up by 13.2 per cent. As a result, the airline showed a net profit of 3.1bn birr. These good results were obtained notwithstanding the many challenges the airline industry had to face. The European Commission's report 'Annual Analysis of the EU Air Transport Market 2016' pointed out the major challenges. According to the analysis, market access restrictions, terrorist attacks, civil strife and disease outbreaks, fuel and taxation-related costs and ever-increasing stiff competition made life more difficult for the airline industry.[2] A challenging global economic environment characterised by slow GDP growth and high oil prices impacted the performance of many airlines. Because of the deterioration of business confidence, the critical premium market segment (business class and first class) slowed down.[3] At the same time, excessive capacity on some routes resulted in a decrease of airfares after adjustment for inflation, and the weakness of the air-cargo industry had led many global airlines to abandon their cargo businesses altogether. In Africa, airlines experienced the slowest demand growth in the world. Capacity growth had been much more important than traffic growth, so African airlines registered a sharp decline in load factors. Another contributing factor was the stiff competition from carriers that were aggressively expanding their route network in Africa. While foreign carriers continued to enjoy good access to the African market, African carriers did not easily obtain traffic rights to important destinations on the continent. It comes as no surprise that many, if not all, of the major African airlines remained in the red – with the exception of Ethiopian Airlines.

On 4 February 2014, the Middle East lessor Palma Holding signed an order for four Bombardier Q400s and four options. The order, placed by Ethiopian Airlines, was valued at US$282m. The new aircraft, which would come in a two-class configuration, would complement Ethiopian's fleet of 13 aircraft of the same type. In the meantime, the airline had taken delivery of a new CAE Q400 full-flight simulator.

On 20 September of the same year, it was revealed Ethiopian Airlines had placed an order for 20 Boeing 737 MAX 8s, with purchase rights for another 15 aircraft of the same type. That year, the airline had already received four 787 Dreamliners, bringing the total number to ten. And it received two 777F aircraft as well. For its Flight Academy, Ethiopian took delivery of three Cessna 172 trainers. A 777-300ER was leased from GE Capital Aviation Services Ltd. As a result, the network was expanded: Qatar, Vienna, Kano (Nigeria) and Shanghai were added. Ethiopian also launched four daily flights to Nairobi and daily flights to London. Its strategic partner, Malawian Airlines, launched its first international service to Johannesburg. Codeshare agreements were signed with ANA, El Al, Malaysian Airways, Air Canada, United Airlines, TAP and Austrian Airlines. In the first weeks of

2015, a codeshare agreement with Air India was expanded, offering air connectivity options between Indian and the African continent via Addis Ababa. Earlier, the airline had already such an agreement for flights between Addis Ababa and both Mumbai and New Delhi. Now the deal was expanded to include, on the one hand, African destinations beyond Addis Ababa and, on the other hand, Chennai, Hyderabad, Ahmedabad and Bengaluru in India. At the same time, Ethiopian was planning to increase its presence in India by offering double daily flights to the country and opening a new route to southern India later that year.

To handle its expanding cargo business, Ethiopian Airlines completed a turnkey contract for the construction of its cargo terminal 2 and apron, with Unitechnik Systems GmbH of Germany. Once completed, the new terminal would be able to accommodate 600,000 tons of cargo per annum, with cargo apron parking capacity for five 747-800 aircraft at a time. The cold storage capacity would amount to 300,000 tons of temperature-controlled perishable cargo per annum. Immediately after completion of terminal 2, a third cargo terminal was planned with the same capacity as the second one.

In line with its pan-African vision, Ethiopian had reportedly been discussing acquiring a strategic stake in government-owned flag carrier RwandAir and launching a new joint venture carrier with the government of South Sudan.[4] The airline had also been discussing the possibility of establishing a joint venture airline in the Democratic Republic of Congo, which would serve as the group's hub for Central Africa. Ethiopian already had a stake in both Togo-based ASKY and Malawian Airlines. ASKY operated a fleet of eight aircraft – three 737-700s and five Dash 8 Q400s, seven of which were owned by Ethiopian. Malawian operated a fleet of one 737-800 and one Dash 8 Q400, both owned by Ethiopian. Including the aircraft of ASKY and Malawian, the Ethiopian group had a fleet of 79 aircraft – more than any other airline group in Africa.

In 2014, Ethiopian Airlines had carried six million passengers. It was one of only four airlines in Africa with over five million passengers. The other African airlines with over five million passengers had recorded virtually zero growth over the last six years. Royal Air Maroc had carried about six million passengers in 2014, whereas South African Airways carried about 7.1 million passengers, maintaining its position as market leader in Africa, based on the number of passengers carried. Egypt Air had carried an estimated seven million passengers. Above all, Ethiopian Airlines was growing much faster than rival Kenya Airways, which had pursued a similar strategy to Ethiopian, expanding in Asia and regionally within Africa but had been set back by instability in its home market.

In 2015, Ethiopian Airlines further expanded by opening up routes to Tokyo and the resumption of flights to Singapore. Tokyo would initially be served with three weekly Boeing 787-800 flights via Hong Kong. With the launch of the new Tokyo route, Hong Kong would be upgraded to a daily non-stop service. Singapore would be served with three weekly non-stop flights by 787-800s. To make this expansion possible, Ethiopian would take delivery of three more Dreamliners in 2015, growing its 787 fleet to 13 aircraft. At the same time, the introduction of Airbus A-350 aircraft was considered.

Los Angeles would become Ethiopian's second destination in the US after Washington Dulles, which was served daily with 777-200LRs. A new codeshare with United Airlines, which was implemented in 2014, would further augment Ethiopian's presence in the United States, as Los Angeles and Dulles are both United Airlines hubs. In Europe, Dublin would become Ethiopian's tenth destination after the addition of Madrid, Stockholm, and Vienna in 2014.

In November 2015, Ethiopian Airlines featured in the news again when it dispatched its first-ever flight operated by an all-female crew. The flight departed from Addis Ababa to Bangkok. On that occasion, Ethiopian's CEO, Tewolde GebreMariam, stated, 'Here in the continent of Africa, we are lagging behind in women empowerment. So, this is going to inspire all the schoolgirls in Africa that they have a very bright future in the 21st century.'[5] The flight was handled by women in every aspect, from planning to aircraft maintenance, from the pilots to air traffic controllers. Ethiopian senior female executives were passengers on board the flight. Earlier, in 2010, Amsale Gualu had become the first Ethiopian Airlines' female captain, flying the Boeing 767. Of course, she was also part of the all-female crew that made the historic flight to Bangkok. On that occasion, she stated, 'When I was in high school, I used to be impressed by the pilots' uniforms. And I guess that is where my passion for flying developed. After graduating from Addis Ababa University, I joined Ethiopian Airlines as first officer on Fokker 50 aircraft. Later, I became captain on the Boeing 767, and now I'm here flying the big Boeing 777.'[6]

Cargo contributed a large part to the excellent results of the airline. This 737-800F is leased from GECAS. (Jozef Mols collection)

Ethiopian Airlines added more Cessna-172s to the Academy's fleet. (Raimund Stehmann)

When Dreamliners arrived, they served African destinations on a rotating basis. (Sander Zwart)

Above: The introduction of the Dreamliner resulted in increased comfort for the airline's passengers. (Sander Zwart)

Below: The introduction of the Dreamliner was not only a giant step forward for Ethiopian, but it also increased the presence of the Star Alliance in Africa. (Sander Zwart)

The 777F is the largest cargo aeroplane in the Ethiopian Airlines fleet. (Sander Zwart)

The first all-female crew. (Ethiopian Airlines via Twitter)

Chapter 8
Zambian Adventure

Running an airline and making a profit is not only a matter of fleets and routes. Customer satisfaction is a very important factor as well. In 2016, Ethiopian Airlines inaugurated the largest and most modern inflight catering centre, covering a total area of 11,500m² and encompassing a modern operations and food-processing area, fully equipped with high-tech cooking and bakery equipment, large capacity dishwashing and heavy-duty ice-cube machines, a hot kitchen, storage units, cold rooms, loading bays, high-lift trucks and vans, a dedicated halal kitchen, as well as a number of modern rooms for the staff.[1]

To further enhance passenger comfort, Ethiopian also introduced the Airbus A350XB on long-term lease from Irish lessor, AerCap. By doing so, the airline became the first African carrier to introduce this new type of aircraft and the first one to fly it in the African skies. During 2016, Ethiopian would receive two of these aircraft. Ethiopian took those planes in a high-density configuration with 343 seats, giving it a significantly higher density option with 27 per cent more seats than its 270-seat Dreamliners. In this way, Ethiopian was in line to have the highest density configuration among the initial A350 operators. Furthermore, the A350-900 has a similar, or slightly longer, range from Addis Ababa than the 787-800.

The A350s made their debut flights to African destinations including Yaoundé, Kigali, Nairobi, Lagos, Bujumbura, Douala, Malabo, Lusaka, Harare, N'Djamena and Entebbe, and they were also used on the route to London. During the 2017 Paris Airshow, Ethiopian announced an additional firm order for ten A350-900s and committed to purchasing two 777 freighter aircraft. The airline also exercised its options for ten 737 MAX 8s. To increase passenger comfort, Ethiopian decided to refurbish its remaining four 767-300 aircraft, which were used on routes to India and the Middle East. While other carriers were retiring this type of aircraft, Ethiopian decided to give the type a second lease of life by installing – among other things – Optimare fully flat ZEST seats and Wi-Fi at an investment of more than US$6m. By doing this, it was hoped the 767 could serve another four years before being replaced by new aircraft on order. One 767 – ET-ALJ – was actually owned by the United Nations (UN) but operated by Ethiopian on its regular and charter services, remaining available for humanitarian missions when needed. It was the only 767 in the UN fleet. Therefore, it would probably remain in the Ethiopian fleet for some time longer. Another 767, painted in Star Alliance livery, also remained in the fleet, as it was still proving its worth.[2] In the meantime, Ethiopian had also installed a full flight simulator for the Boeing B-787 at its main base in Addis Ababa. An Airbus A-350 simulator was also installed.

Obviously, the investments described above were only possible thanks to the financial health of the carrier. In 2015, Ethiopian had made more profit than all other African carriers combined.[3] By 2016, profits had reached US$261.9m compared to US$150.9m the year before, a development attributed to an increase in flight frequencies and the opening up of new routes. Ethiopian's annual report showed the carrier had more than quadrupled its passenger numbers over the past ten years, from 1.76 million passengers in 2005–06 to 7.6 million in 2015–16. And the airline planned to almost treble that again over the next ten years with a forecast of 22 million by 2025. These results were obtained notwithstanding a challenging operating environment caused by a slower global economic performance, the weakening of Africa's major economies, and an Ebola crisis that scared away tourists from African destinations. The airline was also exposed to higher currency fluctuations, leaving more than US$220m of its funds stuck in several African countries that had foreign exchange restrictions. Repatriating funds held up in Nigeria, Egypt, Angola and Sudan as a result of the oil price decline was also a problem, as these countries suffered most by the decreasing income from oil exports. Ethiopian experienced a currency loss of US$18m as a result of continuous currency devaluations in many African countries and the associated problems of profit repatriation. The airline was forced to resort to a natural hedge, making payments in the currency of sales and maintaining a higher cash reserve in stable currencies such as the American dollar, the euro, and the British pound.[4]

The Ethiopian government reorganised the airline as a fully owned aviation holding group in July 2017. The aim was to maximise efficiency, enhance customer services to global standards and ease the long-term planning. The initial group consisted of the Ethiopian Airports Enterprise (EAE), the Passenger Airline Company, Cargo Airline and Logistics Company, the Ethiopian Aviation Academy, Ethiopian Inflight Catering Services, Ethiopian MRO Services and Ethiopian Hotel and Tourism Services. The MRO Services was, at that time, the largest such operation serving the African continent and was fully accredited by the Federal Aviation Administration (FAA) and the European Aviation Safety Agency (EASA). The cargo department was rapidly expanding, thanks to the construction of new and larger facilities. The EAE, however, remained the weak spot of the new holding. Whereas the airline had grown to become an intercontinental airline, offering great value for money, services at the Bole International Airport – Ethiopian's main hub – were below expected standards. It was clear the facilities had become too small to cater for the ever-increasing number of passengers. The training of airport staff was also well below par. Refurbishing existing infrastructure could only offer temporary solutions. Many specialists said the construction of an all-new airport with four runways was the only solution.

To expand its footprint, Ethiopian Airlines entered into some codeshare agreements with Air Namibia and Air Europe. The deal with the Namibian carrier covered Ethiopian's three weekly services to Windhoek, as well as both airlines' services beyond their hubs. The deal with Air Europe, including a free-sale codeshare agreement, thereby allowed the partner airlines access to each other's network by creating smooth connections at their respective hubs. Also, the start-up of new routes was considered, including New York, Chicago and Houston in the US, with a possible stop in Dublin like the Addis Ababa–Dublin–Los Angeles flight, which had performed well since it was launched in 2015. These flights had shown an average load factor of 75 per cent to 80 per cent. In Asia, Ethiopian was planning to further expand in China with additional capacity to Guangzhou and new services to Chengdu. In this way, China would account for almost 10 per cent of Ethiopian's seat capacity. During the airshow in Le Bourget in 2017, Ethiopian announced an order for four 777 freighters, including two aircraft previously on order. Furthermore, the airline also announced an order for ten additional 737 MAX 8 aircraft, exercising options from its 2014 order.

As for its pan-African ambitions, Ethiopian Airlines signed a strategic partnership agreement with the Zambian government to assist in the relaunch of Zambia Airways. Ethiopian would take a 45 per cent stake in the new airline with the rest of the shares held by the Zambian government. This move was aimed at developing Lusaka as an aviation hub for southern Africa and it should be seen in the light of Ethiopian's multiple hub strategy outlined in the 'Vision 2025' strategic plan. Ethiopian was not entering into such joint ventures just for the sake of making money. By expanding the hubs, the airline also contributed significantly to intra-African connectivity. However, in contrast with the ASKY partnership, the co-operation with Zambia soon became a cause for concern. Zambian Airways had been incorporated in 1948, as a subsidiary of Zambia Consolidated Copper Mines. The airline operated two 737-200s as well as two Beechcraft 1900Ds on domestic and regional routes under the trading name of Zambian Airways.[5] On 10 January 2009, the company announced it was suspending operations because of high fuel costs. The Zambian government had to look for another partner airline to start up a new carrier. Therefore, a co-operation deal with Ethiopian could revive the Zambian airline sector. The new carrier would launch operations in October 2018, only for it to be delayed until January 2019. When that deadline was looming, the date was pushed back to April 2019, before the parties involved agreed to, again, push back the launch till the third quarter of 2019. In the end, the launch was scheduled for December 2020. According to *Lusaka Times* (9 September 2020), the government had estimated, before the outbreak of the COVID-19 pandemic, that Zambia's aviation sector was projected to grow at a rate of 13 per cent per annum. Later on, it was stated that the start-up of the airline had to be postponed because of the pandemic causing travel restrictions in Africa. In the meantime, however, Zambia Airways had invested about US$30m for the establishment of the carrier, including the wages of an Ethiopian chief executive officer who lived in Addis Ababa and was running an airline that had not even taken off in Lusaka. In February 2021, Swiss-based ch-aviation revealed that Zambia still intends to launch Zambia Airways and was waiting for the joint-venture partners to decide on a new launch date.[6]

The introduction of the Airbus A350-900 was a milestone for Ethiopian Airlines. (Severin Hackenberger)

The A350-900 was first used on routes to African destinations and to London. (Sander Zwart)

The range of the A350-900 is slightly greater than that of the Dreamliner. (Luca Gussoni)

A business-class cabin onboard the A350-900. (Alberto Ortega)

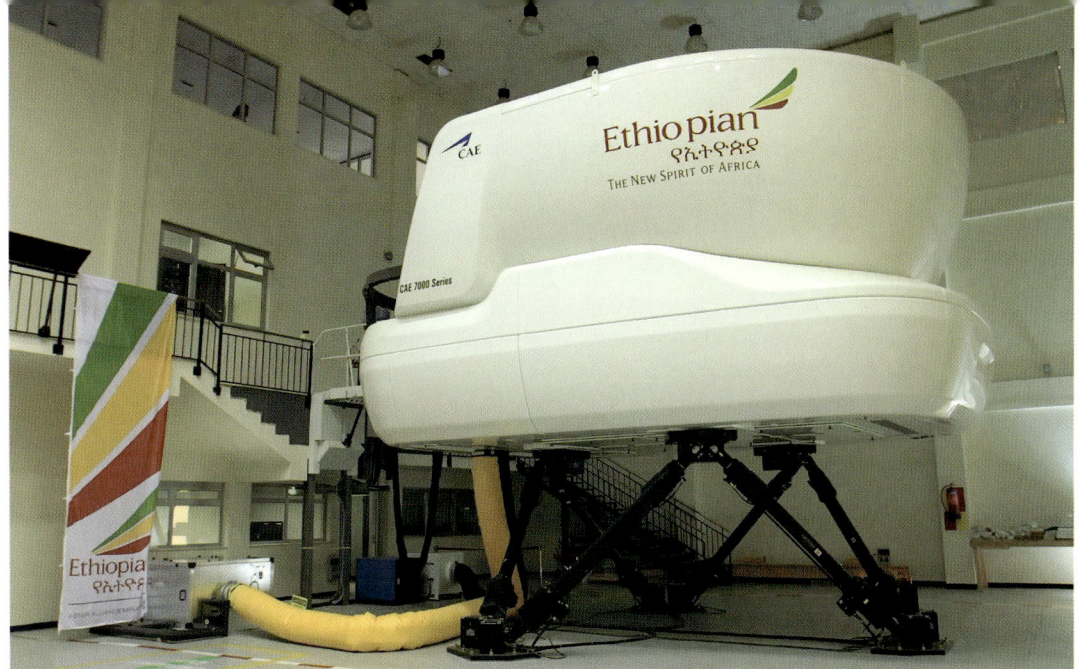

Above: To cater for the arrival of new aircraft, Ethiopian also installed the most modern flight simulators. (Jozef Mols collection)

Right: Some new aircraft in the fleet, like this Dreamliner, proudly showed the Star Alliance colours. (Dong)

Below: Some 767s were refurbished and remained in service, like this one in Star Alliance livery. (Jozef Mols collection)

Part of the Ethiopian Airlines fleet at Bole International Airport. (Jozef Mols collection)

Above left: Besides the comfort of new aircraft, Ethiopian Airlines is also offering perfect inflight service. (Ethiopian Airlines)

Above right: Cabin staff are very well trained by the Ethiopian Academy. (Ethiopian Airlines)

Left: The 100th aircraft of Ethiopian Airlines was a 787-900 Dreamliner. (Chang Li)

Chapter 9
Expanding the African Footprint

Once Ethiopian Airlines had realised that airfreight could be a very profitable business, expanding the cargo department became an important issue. In January 2018, Ethiopian Cargo and Logistics Services signed a lease agreement with lessor GECAS to take the first two Boeing 737-800SF freighters to be converted by Miami, Florida-based Aeronautical Engineers, Inc (AEI). These aircraft would be a great complement to the existing fleet of 777 and 757 freighters. The converted cargo aircraft accommodates 11 full-height containers plus one AEP/AEH and has a main-deck payload of up to 52,000lb. It uses AEI's hydraulically operated cargo door. The leasing of these two Boeings was in line with the 'Vision 2025' strategic plan, as it allowed the expansion of the cargo fleet network and supported trade within Africa and with the rest of the world by facilitating the export of perishables and the import of high-value goods into the continent. The delivery of the converted aircraft (using passenger aircraft) was scheduled for June 2018 and January 2019. In the meantime, the list of cargo destinations had grown to a daily uplift capacity standing at 650 tonnes. Under the 'Vision 2025' strategic plan it is the intention to service 57 cargo points with a fleet of 18 aircraft, having the capacity to uplift 1.5 million tonnes annually.

To further increase its African footprint, Ethiopian Airlines added Nosy Be as a second destination in Madagascar, after Antananarivo. The thrice-weekly service is an outbound extension of the existing connection to the Comoros with a direct return to Addis Ababa. Kisangani and Mbuji-Mayi in the Democratic Republic of Congo were also added to the network, bringing the total number of points served in Africa to 58.

Ethiopian Airlines' rapid expansion in Africa was, in part, made possible because of the signature of the Single African Air Transport Market (SAATM) agreement in January 2018. The primary goal of SAATM is to fully implement the 1999 Yamoussoukro Decision. Under this agreement, all participants agreed to lift market access restrictions for airlines, remove restrictions on ownership, grant each other extended air traffic rights (first through fifth freedoms) and liberalise flight frequency and capacity limits.[1] Both passenger and cargo aviation are included in the agreement. Oversight over the SAATM is exercised by the African Union, its Regional Economic Communities, and the African Civil Aviation Commission (AFCAC).[2] The benefits of liberalising such traffic was first stressed in Yamoussoukro, but the implementation of the agreement faced many obstacles, as regulatory bodies, necessary for the implementation, did not become operational. It would last until 28 January 2018, when Rwandan President Paul Kagame, as the new chairperson of the African Union, launched SAATM. Twenty-three member states of the African Union originally agreed to join SAATM as starting participants.[3] By March 2020, this number had increased to 33 countries. As is often the case, SAATM received both criticism and support.[4] The African Development Bank predicted that SAATM would lead to cheaper flights, greater passenger volumes and economic benefits. However, some African governments (such as the Ugandan government) and some smaller airlines criticised the project. They alleged the agreement would lead to a few big airlines dominating the market, thus stifling competition. Abdérahmane Berthé, the secretary general of the African Airlines Association, would later state that

Safety training with the Ethiopian Aviation Academy. (Ethiopian Airlines)

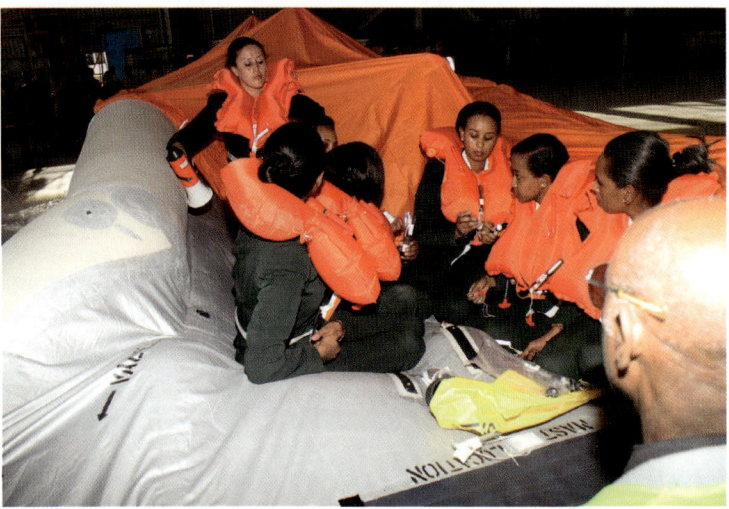

These future cabin crew members learn how to survive in the event of a water landing. (Ethiopian Airlines)

Cabin crews from other airlines also receive their training at the Ethiopian Airlines facility. (Ethiopian Airlines)

Chapter 10
'Pitch Up, Pitch Up'

While Ethiopian was rapidly expanding its influence across Africa, things at home were also going well. In April 2018, a planned aerospace manufacturing facility was announced. There was already the small existing unit under Ethiopian MRO Services, that manufactured wire harnesses for Boeing. The new division, a joint venture with Aerosud of South Africa, would be capable of designing and manufacturing aircraft parts for plane makers. Negotiations were started with Boeing, Honeywell, Airbus and Bombardier Aerospace among others in search of clients. Accreditation would be sought from the FAA and EASA. The needed human resources would be secured from the local technical schools and higher learning institutions.[1] The same year, Ethiopian Airlines signed an agreement with the German-based ACM Aerospace to set up a facility that would manufacture and supply aircraft seat covers, safety belts, carpets and other interior parts.

However, Ethiopian Airlines' history would also know some black pages. On 10 March 2019, Flight ET 302 – a 737 MAX 8 – took off from Bole International Airport in Addis Ababa for a scheduled flight to Jomo Kenyatta International Airport in Nairobi. Six minutes after the start, the plane crashed, killing all 157 people on board (149 passengers and eight crew members).[2] The aircraft was only four months old and had accrued 1,200 flight hours. It had been maintained on 4 February 2019. ABC7 New York Eyewitness News covered the complete timeline of the disaster. The plane took off at 08.38. Records shared by Flightradar24 showed that the plane's vertical speed quickly became erratic.[3] Shortly afterwards, the pilots issued a distress call and decided to return to the airport. A cockpit warning device on board the doomed flight was heard saying 'Pitch up, pitch up' moments before the crash. According to the *Wall Street Journal*, the plane's nose began to pitch down as the jet reached an altitude of 450ft. It also reported that pilot Ahmed Nur Mohammed radioed the control tower to report a 'flight control problem' and wrestled to level the plane's flight path.[4] There were immediate fears that anti-stalling technology on board the new plane might have played a role in the disaster. Some suggested the manoeuvring characteristics augmentation system played a key role. Earlier, in October 2018, a plane of the same type had been involved in a similar accident in Indonesia, claiming the life of 189 people.

As a result of the accident, several airlines and aviation authorities chose to temporarily suspend the use of the 737 MAX 8 aircraft. On 12 March, EASA recommended closing the airspace in Europe to aircraft of this type. Just before, the Civil Aviation Authority itself had introduced such a ban in Norway. Norwegian, the only operator of the type in Norway, had already decided to keep all its 737 MAX aircraft on the ground. The Ethiopian Accident Investigation Bureau sent the flight data recorder (FDR) and the cockpit voice recorder (CVR) to the French accident investigation agency, BEA, for analysis. Later, Wossenyeleh Hunegaw – the director general of the Ethiopian Civil Aviation Authority – told AINonline (21 March 2019) that 'based on the readings of the CVR and FDR, it was confirmed that there were clear similarities between the Indonesian Lion Air Flight 610 and Ethiopian Airlines ET302 accidents.'[5] The flight path, altitude, flight time and speed of the two 737 MAX 8 aircraft were similar.

In July 2017, the Reuters press agency announced that Boeing was willing to pay US$100m to the 737 MAX crash victims in Indonesia and Ethiopia. However, the funds would not go directly to the families of the victims. Instead, the money would be paid to local governments and non-profit organisations that could help families and communities gain education and jobs. At the time of this press release, Boeing was facing dozens of lawsuits from victims' families. Many of them refused to agree to a separate settlement with the aircraft manufacturer. In the meantime, the FAA had identified a new and, as yet, unresolved problem with the MAX aircraft.

To streamline all individual lawsuits in American courts of justice by family members of the victims, the Chicago Federal Courthouse overseeing litigation related to both the Lion Air and Ethiopian Airlines crashes ordered all Ethiopian Airlines crash cases in the United States Federal Court in Chicago to be consolidated into a single proceeding. This would streamline the hearings and maybe lead to additional discoveries. In July 2019, Weisberg & Sims filed a lawsuit against Boeing seeking punitive damages for violations of the Illinois Consumer Fraud and Deceptive Business Practices Act.[6] The lawsuit detailed the history of the development of the 737 MAX 8 and detailed alleged fraud, deception and misrepresentations made by Boeing to rush the 737 MAX 8 to the market in its 'competition war' with Airbus. The lawyers stated that, 'Boeing chose to advance a corporate culture that emphasized development speed and profits over safety, knowing that the proliferation of such corporate culture would drive enormous corporate profits, but significantly increase the risk of an aviation disaster resulting in catastrophic loss of life.' At the same time, a joint investigation by the US Department of Justice and the US Department of Transportation Inspector General's Office looked into the circumstances surrounding the certification of the 737 MAX. It concluded that, in recent years, the FAA had shifted more authority over the approval of new aircraft to the manufacturer itself, even allowing Boeing to choose many of the personnel who oversee tests and vouch for aircraft safety.[7, 8]

After Boeing had been charged with conspiracy to defraud the United States, the manufacturer agreed not to contest the charges and admitted that it had engaged in criminal conduct intended to deceive and mislead the FAA during the 737 MAX certification process. Under the terms of the agreement with the Justice Department, Boeing will pay a total criminal monetary amount of over US$2.5bn, composed of a criminal monetary penalty of US$234m, compensation payments to 737 MAX airline customers of US$1.77bn and the establishment of a US$500m crash victim beneficiaries fund to compensate the heirs, relatives and legal beneficiaries of the 346 passengers who died in the crashes of Lion Air and Ethiopian Airlines.[9] The agreement does not cover any misconduct of Boeing's top corporate officials, although it highlights the conduct of the Boeing test pilots who chose to repeatedly mislead the FAA.

Immediately after the agreement with the Justice Department, the US attorneys representing Ethiopian Airlines in their case against Boeing advised the airline to not accept the settlement on offer. In their opinion, the US$500m offered by Boeing was not enough, as it was just a 'mere fraction' of the actual damages to the airline in terms of both physical loss and damage to the brand's reputation. Levitt Gutzler, co-founding partner of the attorney's office, encouraged GebreMariam to 'reject Boeing's current, desperate settlement entreaties' and immediately file and prosecute its claims against Boeing in the United States.[10, 11, 12] Actually, Gutzler suggested to claim approximately US$1.8bn. However, one has to take into account that the US legal system can run painfully slowly, particularly in cases involving large corporations of national interest. For Ethiopian, taking Boeing to court might mean a lead time of years, not months, before the compensation is in the bank account. Of course, the high cost of hiring attorneys has to also be considered. Although no exact figures are known, one can imagine the attorneys are billing amounts in the region of US$500 to US$600 per hour! Finally, there is also the fact that Boeing often 'pays' damages by way of discounts on future purchases.

In the meantime, Ethiopian Airlines – like many other airlines worldwide – had to ground all 737 MAX aircraft in the fleet, and it also had to decide whether to cancel outstanding orders for more aircraft of the same type. In the past, other airlines had cancelled their orders for the MAX aircraft. Ethiopian had experienced a tragic accident, and it was proved beyond reasonable doubt that the cause of the accident was the design defect of the aircraft. However, after changes to the type, the FAA in the US and EASA in Europe cleared the plane. Experts, technicians, engineers and pilots had been satisfied that the modifications would address the flight control systems that had created the problems with the aircraft. Therefore, Ethiopian Airlines decided to continue operating the MAX. However, it was made clear that Ethiopian would not be among the first carriers to fly the aeroplane, because the airline had been severely affected by the accident and it would take time to convince passengers the aircraft was safe.

Above: The MRO department is rapidly expanding. (Ethiopian Airlines)

Right: The MRO department performs engine maintenance for aircraft in the Ethiopian fleet but also for other African carriers. (Raimund Stehmann)

The MRO department at work. (Raimund Stehmann)

Arrival of a 737 MAX 8 in Ethiopia. (Jozef Mols collection)

Above: With the arrival of the 737 MAX 8, Ethiopian would experience one of its major accidents. (Jozef Mols collection)

Below: This photograph shows the doomed 737 MAX 8. (Wikimedia Commons/LLGB Spotters)

This is all that remains of the crashed 737 MAX 8 (Ethiopian Civil Aviation Authority on Twitter)

The crash of the 737 MAX 8 would be the start of a series of court cases against Boeing in the US and the worldwide grounding of the type. (Ethiopian Civil Aviation Authority on Twitter)

Crash site of the Boeing 737 MAX 8. (Ethiopian Civil Aviation Authority on Twitter)

This 737 MAX 8 (minus winglets) is awaiting possible delivery to Ethiopian Airlines after the crash of another Ethiopian aircraft of the same type. (Haofeng Yu)

Chapter 11
The COVID-19 Pandemic

While Ethiopian Airlines was recovering from the 737 MAX 8 crash and its consequences, the airline had to face another major disaster. Once again, the origin of the problems was not located within Ethiopia or Africa. While the Boeing accident found its origins in Seattle, the COVID-19 pandemic started – probably – in a small market somewhere in China. At first, the disease was considered to be 'another type of flu, caused by a mutation of the virus'. Every day, newspapers reported some 'ten to twenty' new cases of COVID infections within China or other Asian countries. Even government leaders – notably the US president – stressed there was no reason to panic and there was even less reason to close down the economy or the social life of its subjects. However, slowly at first, and then faster and faster, the epidemic started to spread. Some leaders and managers of larger corporations still hoped the pandemic would be contained to one continent like the SARS epidemic of 2003, which started with an outbreak in China and spread to only four other Asian countries. However, this epidemic also showed a clear capacity to spread along the routes of international air travel.[1] In 2012, the Middle East respiratory syndrome coronavirus (MERS-CoV) pandemic had spread throughout the Middle East, Africa and some Asian countries. In the case of COVID-19, it seemed the virus started spreading much faster than had been the case with previous respiratory diseases. By the end of March 2020, governments decided to limit air travel or completely close some of its airports. Like other airlines around the world, Ethiopian Airlines also had to face this new challenge.

Whenever the airlines start to recover from the COVID-19 crisis, the way uphill for these carriers will start much further down the mountain. Most airlines were already loss-making before the pandemic and are ill-equipped for the tough journey that will continue for a long time.[2] Africa makes up 20.3 per cent of the world's landmass, but African airlines carry only 2.1 per cent of world airline traffic. By comparison, Europe has 6.7 per cent landmass and 26.8 per cent of world airline traffic. Adbérahmane Berthé, the secretary general of the African Airlines Association, made the situation clear in an interview with Aviation Week Network (25 November 2020). He stated that before COVID-19, African airlines were losing money and that COVID has only aggravated this situation, so that they lose even more money. At the same time, Africa was also facing a connectivity crisis. Before the pandemic, the continent had sparse connections and many of them remain closed because of COVID-related issues. The Air Transport Action Group (ATAG) estimated that 4.5 million African aviation jobs (out of a total of 7.7 million) were at risk.[3] All countries closed their borders, meaning African airlines were grounded from March 2020 until September 2020. With no bailout funding available, the airline industry was severely damaged. During the first peak in the COVID-19 pandemic, the Coronavirus levels in Africa was not that bad at all. However, with African sub-standard health services, the fear existed that African countries would not be able to support a growing number of pandemic patients. Therefore, Ethiopian Airlines could no longer operate passenger services to some 20 airports owing to bans on entry, border closures, passenger quarantines and decreased demand.

Ethiopian Airlines, however, could see that there was an opportunity with cargo demand, and it made a very quick decision to build up its capacity. This helped the airline to manage its cash flow without any bailout money or borrowing and without any lay-offs or salary reductions.[4]

Over the years, Ethiopian was able to build up a lot of experience in the field of air cargo. (Ethiopian Airlines)

Besides standard cargo, Ethiopian is used to transport humanitarian aid all over the African continent. (Ethiopian Airlines)

A cargo plane is being unloaded. (Ethiopian Airlines)

Left: When the COVID-19 pandemic hit the world, Ethiopian Airlines was ready for a quick response. (Ethiopian Airlines)

Below: Ethiopian's Pharma Wing is specialised in medical cold-chain routes to transport temperature-controlled medicines, including COVID-19 vaccines. (Ethiopian Airlines)

This Dash Q400 was quickly converted to transport freight. (Ethiopian Airlines)

By removing seats, passenger planes were converted for the transportation of medical supplies. (Ethiopian Airlines)

Above: Passenger jets were converted for the transportation of urgent cargo. (Ethiopian Airlines)

Right: Urgent cargo inside the cabin of a passenger jet. (Ethiopian Airlines)

Left: Inside the hold of a cargo plane. (Ethiopian Airlines)

Below: Obviously, the cabin crew must wear face masks during the COVID-19 pandemic. (Ethiopian airlines)

Appendix 1
Incidents and Accidents

(Based upon information from the Aviation Safety Network)

On 22 July 1948, a Douglas C-47A (ET-T-5) overran the wet runway at Gore Airport. The pilot intentionally ground-looped the aeroplane. It skidded into rocks, causing the right undercarriage to collapse. The fuselage was later turned in to the Ethiopian Airlines office at the Gore Airport. There were no fatalities.

On 17 July 1957, a Lockheed L-749 Constellation (ET-T-35) on an international flight from Athens, via Khartoum, to Addis Ababa experienced an inflight fire in the No 2 engine. The engine was feathered, and the CO_2 bottle was fired. An explosion occurred, however, followed by a violent fire. The crew made a gear-up forced landing on a large, flat cultivated area some 30 miles from Khartoum Airport. The aircraft skidded for 1,020ft before coming to a stop. Just before the forced landing, at a height of 1,000ft, the No 2 engine had dropped clear of the aircraft, causing severe buffeting and sharp lowering of the left wing. The probable cause was determined as overheating of the main landing gear's brakes during the aircraft's taxiing and take-off run in Khartoum for the second leg of the flight. It was caused by a dragging brake and a leakage of hydraulic fluids with a resultant fire and tyre blow out. The tyre blow out resulted in damage to hydraulic oil and fuel lines within the confined area of the No 2 nacelle, between the rear spars and between the fuselage and left side of the landing-gear wheel doors. There were no fatalities.

On 15 July 1960, a Douglas C-47A (ET-T-18) crashed into mountainous terrain, at 9,400ft altitude, 17.1 miles south of Jimma. The aircraft was flying the Bulchi–Jimma route and carrying eight passengers plus a cargo of coffee. After contacting Jimma, the pilot requested that the Jimma non-directional beacon (NDB) be turned on. There was no further contact with the flight. The accident was caused by the pilot, who misjudged the weather and continued to fly into deteriorating meteorological conditions, while trying to maintain visual flight rules (VFR). He attempted to climb at a speed well below the minimum safe climb speed of the aircraft. One crew member died in the accident.

On 5 September 1961, a Douglas C-47A (ET-T-16) on a charter survey flight for American Coronado Petroleum Corporation experienced a propeller malfunction. The pilot tried to return to Addis Ababa, but the aircraft crashed south of Sendafa. Of the 19 occupants, five perished.

On 13 January 1962, a Douglas C-47A (ET-T-1) took off at Tippi Airport on a scheduled domestic flight to Jimma. The aircraft swerved on take-off and crashed into a mill after striking some people nearby. A young girl died and three people on the ground were seriously injured. Of the 18 occupants, five perished. The aircraft was damaged beyond repair.

On 30 November 1963, a Douglas C-47A (ET-AAT) banked to the left on take-off and swerved off the runway. The aircraft was on a test flight following overhaul, and it appeared that the aileron cables were cross connected. There were no fatalities.

On 10 January 2015, a Boeing 737-400F (ET-AQV), flying a cargo flight on behalf of ASKY, sustained substantial damage in a runway excursion on landing at the Accra Kotoka Airport in Ghana. The three crew members were taken to hospital. At the time of the crash, the local weather station and the METAR issuing system had been offline since 6 January 2015, but it is not clear if weather conditions caused the accident.

On 10 March 2019, a four-month-old Boeing 737 MAX 8 (ET-AVJ) crashed near Bishoftu six minutes after take-off from Bole International Airport. The flight was en route to Nairobi. All 157 occupants were killed. This was the first of two accidents with an aircraft of that type, causing the worldwide grounding of the type and the cancellation of its certification.

On 22 July 2020, a Boeing 777F (ET-ARH) caught fire on the ground at Shanghai Pudong International Airport. Nobody was hurt.

Appendix 2
Ethiopian Airlines Fleet Details

(based on information received from the airline and from Planespotters.net)

Aircraft Type	Total	First Introduction	Last Removed	Notes
Douglas DC-3/C-47	18	1946	1991	
Convair 240	3	1950	?	
Lockheed Constellation	1	1957	1957	Scrapped after accident
Douglas DC 6B	3	1958	?	
Boeing 720B	5	1963	?	
Boeing 707-320	2	1968	?	
DHC Dash 7	5	1975	?	
Boeing 727	3	1979	?	
DHC Buffalo	2	1982	1997	
DHC Twin Otter	5	1985	?	
Boeing 767-200	3	May 1984	October 2007	
Boeing 737-200	3	1 December 1987	1 September 2008	
Lockheed Hercules	2	1988	2013	
Boeing 757-200PF	1	August 1990	June 2018	
Boeing 757-200	10	1 November 1991	1 April 2016	
ATR 42	3	July 1996	June 2000	Two scrapped, one leased to Air Botswana
Boeing 767-300	12	July 1996	–	Still in use
Fokker 50	5	1 September 1996	May 2014	
Boeing 737-700	7	March 2004	1 April 2018	
McDonnell Douglas MD11	3	July 2006	1 April 2015	
Boeing 757-200F	1	October 2006	October 2017	
Boeing 737-800	21	March 2009	–	Still in use
Boeing 777-200	6	1 November 2010	–	Still in use
Bombardier DHC8-400	31	1 December 2010	–	Still in use
Boeing 787-800	19	August 2012	–	Still in use

Aircraft Type	Total	First Introduction	Last Removed	Notes
Boeing 777-300ER	5	1 November 2013	–	Still in use
Boeing 777F	9	October 2014	–	Still in use
Airbus A350-900	16	June 2016	–	Still in use
Boeing 787-900	8	October 2017	–	Still in use
Boeing 737 MAX 8	5	1 November 2018		One crashed, four parked at Boeing pending agreement
Boeing 737-800F		March 2019		Still in use

Appendix 3
Notes and References

Chapter 1
1. Dwyer-Lindgren, Jeremy, 'Ethiopian Airlines: From Humble Beginnings to an Aviation Powerhouse', NYC Aviation.com (11 July 2014)
2. Tücker, Phillip Thomas, 'The Legacy of the Brown Condor', *Selamta,* Ethiopian Airlines' inflight magazine (March–April 2016)
3. 'John Charles Robinson', EFAN- Ethiopia (May 2015)
4. 'Second Italo-Ethiopian War', en.wikipedia.org

Chapter 2
1. "Ethiopian Airlines History", Corporate Ethiopian Airlines
2. Mols, Josef, 'Ethiopian Airlines, An Aviation Powerhouse", Key.Aero.com (15 November 2018)
3. 'Glorious Pilots', Glorious pilots book series on Facebook.com (20 September 2016)
4. Dwyer-Lindgren, Jeremy, "Ethiopian Airlines: From Humble Beginnings to an Aviation Powerhouse", NYC Aviation.com (11 July 2014)
5. 'Ethiopian Airlines", en.wikipedia.org
6. 'Glorious Pilots – 8th April 1946: The First Scheduled Flight", de.de.facebook (20 September 2016)

Chapter 3
1. "Ethiopian Airlines', en.wikipedia.org
2. 'Ethiopian Airlines', en.wikipedia.org
3. 'EAA Still Giving a Helping Hand to Africa', African Aerospace.aero (25 August 2017)
4. 'Case Studies from Africa: Air Transport Services, A Case Study of Ethiopia', African Union/UNDP (December 2015)
5. 'Ethiopian Airlines", en.wikipedia.org
6. 'Ethiopia', en.wikipedia.org

Chapter 4
1. 'Ethiopian Airlines: a Proud History', *Selamta*, Ethiopian Airlines' inflight magazine (19 May 2011)
2. '1983–1985 Famine in Ethiopia', en.wikipedia.org
3. 'Ethiopian Civil War', en.wikipedia.org
4. Price, Alfred, 'Ethiopian Birthday', FlightGlobal.com (24 April 1996)
5. 'Ethiopian Airlines', en.wikipedia.org

Chapter 5
1. Bekele, Kaleyesus, 'Seasoned Aviation Guru Speaks about Ethiopian Airlines', *The Reporter, Ethiopia* (17 November 2018)
2. 'Ethiopian Airlines and ASKY Sign a Management Contract', Corporate Ethiopian Airlines (16 January 2009)
3. 'Ethiopian Signs Code Share Deal with Air China', Corporate Ethiopian Airlines (15 December 2010)

Chapter 6
1. 'Air Malawi under Liquidation', IOL News.co.za (16 November 2012)

Chapter 7
1. 'Ethiopian the Largest Airline in Africa', Corporate Ethiopian Airlines (September 2016)
2. 'Annual Analyses of the EU Air Transport Market 2016', European Commission (28 March 2017)
3. 'Ethiopian Airlines Annual Report 2013/14', Ethiopian Airlines.com. (October 2021)
4. 'Ethiopian Airlines 2015 Outlook: More Rapid Expansion as it Becomes Africa's Largest Airline', CAPA Centre for Aviation.com (13 January 2015)
5. Chartora, Arthur, 'All-Female Flight Crew Operate Ethiopian Airlines' Inaugural Buenos Aires Flight', This is Africa.me (9 March 2018)
6. 'Ethiopian Airlines Pilot who Led All-Female Intra-African Flight Happy over Feat', How Africa.com (March 2018)

Chapter 8
1. 'Ethiopia Inaugurates the Largest and Most Modern Inflight Catering Centre', Corporate Ethiopian Airlines (27 October 2016)
2. Bailey, Joanna, 'Ethiopia is Phasing Out The Boeing 767 But May Keep Some – Here's Why', Simple Flying.com (1 September 2020)
3. Mwanza, Kevin, 'Ethiopian Airlines Make More Profit Than All Other African Carriers Combined', The Moguldom Nation.com (24 August 2015)
4. Olingo, Allan, 'Ethiopian Carrier Flies High, Doubling Profits', The East African.co.ke (6 September 2017)
5. 'Zambian Airways", en.wikipedia.org.
6. 'Amid Delays, Lusaka Still Keen to Launch Zambia Airways', ch-aviation.com (17 February 2021)

Chapter 9
1. Schlumberger, Charles E, 'Open Skies in Africa – Implementing the Yamoussoukro Decision', Washington, DC, The World Bank (2010)
'Declaration of Yamoussoukro on an new African Air Transport Policy', UN Economic Commission for Africa (October 1988) 'SAATM States', AFCAC Executing Agency (November 2018)
2. Aglionby, John, 'Twenty-three African states launch single aviation market', *Financial Times*, Addis Ababa (January 2018)

3. Bekele, Kaleyesus, 'Africans Still Divided on a Single Air Transport Market', AINonline.com (30 January 2018)
4. Bekele, Kaleyesus, 'Nigeria to Turn over Management of Arik to Ethiopian Airlines', AINonline.com (23 August 2017)
5. Bekele, Kaleyesus, 'Ethiopia Ends Negotiations to Manage Arik Air', AINonline.com (26 December 2017)
6. 'Ethiopian Airlines Steps up Hunt for African Connections', Africanews.com (24 November 2018)
7. 'Ethiopian Airlines to Partner Air Djibouti', Horn Diplomat.com (11 October 2017)

Chapter 10

1. 'Ethiopian Airlines', en.wikipedia.org
2. 'Ethiopian Airlines Flight 302', en.wikipedia.org
3. The Associated Press, 'Timeline of the Deadly Ethiopian Airlines Crash', Federal News Network.com (10 March 2019)
4. Mee, Emily, 'Pitch Up, Pitch Up: the Final Moments of Ethiopian Airlines Plane Crash', Sky News.com (31 March 2019)
5. Bekele, Kaleyesus, 'Ethiopia to Fast Track Report into 737 MAX Crash', AINonline.com (21 March 2019)
6. 'Boeing 737 MAX 8 Lawsuits: Over Three Decades of Commercial Aviation Experience', Rapoport Weisberg & Sims PC (7 January 2021)
7. 'Airplane Manufacturer Charged with Conspiracy to Defraud FAA and Agrees to Pay over $2.5 billion', Investigation Office of the Inspector General, US Department of Transportation, Eric J. Soskin, Inspector General (7 January 2021)
8. 'The Boeing 737 MAX: Examining the Federal Aviation Administration's Oversight of the Aircraft's Certification', House Transportation and Infrastructure Committee, Congress.gov, (11 December 2019)
9. Shepardson, David, 'Exclusive: U.S. Opens $500 Million Fund for Relatives of Boeing 737 MAX Victims', Reuters.com (24 June 2021)
10. 'Lawyers advise Ethiopian Airlines against "financially disastrous" settlement offer by Boeing over 737 MAX crash', *The Seattle Times* (21 January 2021)
11. Bailey, Joanna, 'Ethiopian Airlines Urged to Reject 737 MAX Compensation Offer', Simple Flying.com (22 January 2021)
12. 'Lawyers advise Ethiopian not to settle with Boeing', ch-aviation.com (26 January 2021)

Chapter 11

1. 'Severe Acute Respiratory Syndrome (SARS)', World Health Organization.int (16 November 2002)
2. Moores, Victoria, 'Analysis: For most African Carriers, Next Year Will Be Precarious', Aviation Week.com (25 November 2020)
3. '4.5 Million African Jobs at Risk due to COVID-19 and Travel Restrictions', IATA.org (1 October 2020)
4. Harper, Lewis, 'Tewolde Gebremariam – Ethiopian Airlines', FlightGlobal.com (2 February 2021)
5. Bailey, Joanna, 'Ethiopian Begins Refitting Makeshift Freight 777s With Seats', Simple Flying.com, (28 August 2020)

6. Olander, Eric Claude, 'Ethiopian Airlines Gambles With its Hardwon Brand Equity by Continuing to Fly to China', The ChinaAfrica Project.com (5 February 2020)
7. Darros, Remy, 'Ethiopian Airlines to China: last international carrier standing', The Africa Report.com (27 March 2020)
8. 'France Suspends Ethiopian Airlines Flights for Four Days', Le Journal de l'Aviation.com, (28 January 2021)